D1311507

GREAT CAREERS IN THE SPORTS INDUSTRY™

DREAM JOBS
IN SPORTS
FINANCE
AND
ADMINISTRATION

MARTY GITLIN

ROSEN
PUBLISHING®

New York

Rosen Publishing
Published in 2015 by The Rosen Publishing Group, Inc.
29 East 21st Street, New York, NY 10010
Copyright © 2015 by The Rosen Publishing Group, Inc.

First Edition

All rights reserved. No part of this book may be reproduced in any form without permission in writing from the publisher, except by a reviewer.

Library of Congress Cataloging-in-Publication Data

Gitlin, Marty.
Dream jobs in sports finance and administration/Marty Gitlin.
    pages cm.—(Great careers in the sports industry)
Includes bibliographical references and index.
ISBN 978-1-4777-7520-2 (library bound)
1. Sports administration—Vocational guidance. 2. Sports—Finance—Vocational guidance. I. Title.
GV713.G57 2014
796.069—dc23
                                                    2013038936

Manufactured in the United States of America

CONTENTS

The signing of free agents is a key component to sports finance. Superstar quarterback Peyton Manning is seen here between Denver Broncos owner Pat Bowlen (*left*) and general manager John Elway.

The excitement of sports is no longer played out exclusively on the baseball diamond, football field, or basketball court. It extends beyond the soccer stadium, golf course, or skating rink. In this age of multimillion-dollar contracts for athletes and billion-dollar income streams for professional teams and college programs, much of the drama is acted out behind closed doors. The media conveys as much information and opinion about the economics of sports as they do about the action that takes place between the lines.

Those who deal with the financial realities of modern athletics have become critically important to their employers. This action beyond the action that takes place on the field or court includes many lines of work in a wide variety of athletics and at all levels of competition.

5

The sports world boasts thousands of employees who are vital to the economic well-being of a professional franchise or the athletic programs of schools and community organizations. Some negotiate lucrative deals with professional stars. Others maximize revenue at the college level by attracting corporate partnerships. Still others plan simple fund-raisers for the local high school athletic department or youth events. And for every person responsible for those essential tasks, there are dozens who work in other areas of sports economics and finance.

Despite the wide array of tasks embraced by those in sports finance and administration, each staff member is part of a team. Those dealing in the financial aspects of youth sports or organizations must work in harmony to maximize the experience for participants. Those toiling in the economics of high school or college athletic departments or professional sports franchises must understand that the ultimate goal of their employers is to attract and retain paying fans.

Creating winning teams or signing premier athletes in individual sports is essential when attempting to generate ticket sales. The competition for top performers is intense. Those who recruit and offer scholarships to potential college standouts or negotiate contracts for professional stars play critical roles in the success or failure of an athletic program or franchise.

The tasks of those who work in the world of sports finance and administration are made far easier when they are part of a winning organization. But they, too, must perform well, whether they work in sales, marketing, or promotions. Fans attending sports events now expect to be entertained beyond game action in this modern era of sports. They expect Wi-Fi connectivity; participatory fan zones, contests, and giveaways; and lounges that feature food, drink, and big-screen televisions showing dozens of other sporting events. Employees in finance and their colleagues in administration and advertising/marketing work in harmony to create a game-day experience that will entice fans to abandon their couches and head to the stadium or arena.

Though "major sports" such as Major League Baseball, professional and college football, basketball, and ice hockey grab most of the attention in the United States, the far wider world of athletic activities provide nearly unlimited possibilities for those seeking a career in sports finance and administration. National and even international sports organizations abound that require a strong financial and administrative structure to thrive. Such organizations include those that run events such as the Summer and Winter Olympics and oversee sports such as tennis and golf on both professional and amateur levels. Organizations in charge of sports such as horse racing and auto racing also require the skills and knowledge of financial experts. Local and state organizations seek employees to contribute to economic health in such youth sports as gymnastics, soccer, Pop Warner football, and Little League Baseball and Softball.

This book will examine the most prominent jobs in the realm of sports finance and administration. It will explain how these positions are critical to running sports organizations, facilities, and the events themselves. It will also delve into the most effective paths to securing work in the field and the benefits of making it a career. After all, the talented and fortunate few who become professional athletes are not the only people who experience the excitement, joy, and financial rewards of the sports business.

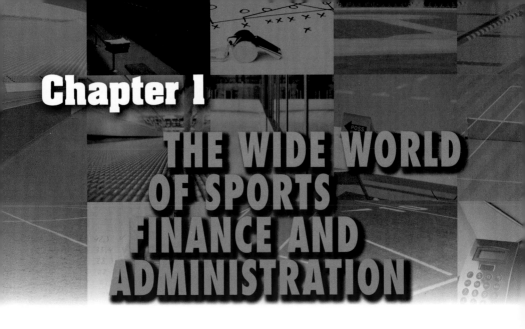

Chapter 1

THE WIDE WORLD OF SPORTS FINANCE AND ADMINISTRATION

From the tiniest township baseball and soccer fields in neighborhoods throughout America to the spectacular one-hundred-thousand-seat college and professional football stadiums, sports teams and individual athletes entertain excited fans every day. They offer a diversion for millions of people struggling with personal and professional problems. They provide a rooting interest and connect generations through cherished experiences and memories. They thrill fans with their skills and passion for the games in which they compete.

Whether it is the trickle of parents walking to the park to watch their daughters play Little League softball, tens of thousands of students and alumni streaming in to watch a showdown between college basketball rivals, or one hundred million hard-core fans and casual viewers alike tuning in to the Super Bowl on network television, sports is an obsession in North America. Anyone

Attracting fans is one important task of any sports franchise. Fans here are streaming into the Cincinnati Reds' Great American Ball Park to watch the Reds play the Milwaukee Brewers.

seeking a nonplaying job in the world of athletics must understand that they are providing a service to their communities and even their country. Personal satisfaction should extend beyond earning a paycheck to include the sheer joy of working together with colleagues to bring happiness to those for whom sports mean so much.

The notion that one is working hard to make life better for others is common to many jobs. But it is particularly relevant to those working in finance and administration at the larger high school, major college, and professional sports levels. After all, sports finance employees are part of a team that provides entertainment for thousands and sometimes millions of fans. They are responsible for attracting and serving the athletes whose talents bring in revenue to schools, communities, and professional franchises.

AN ATHLETIC DIRECTOR AT WORK

University of Alabama Athletic Director Bill Battle is the financial steward of his department. He is driven to achieve the most efficient use of his budget. But his job description goes far beyond the economic realm. He understands his duty to the school and to those who play sports for the Crimson Tide. He knows that one good deed leads to another. If he performs with zeal and effectiveness in serving University of Alabama athletes, they will be better motivated to maximize their talents. That leads to winning, which leads to ticket and merchandise sales, advertising revenue, and lucrative corporate partnerships. And that results in higher income for the university and its athletic department.

It is a simple equation for Battle. He believes that if he treats people with the respect they deserve and does his job effectively, all else falls into place. But he also knows that it takes a special personality to do his job well. "It helps greatly to be a people person, at least in the sense that you have to love people to be a good leader," Battle

University of Alabama athletic director Bill Battle oversees one of the top programs in America. He is shown here speaking to the media upon his introduction as AD in March 2013.

explained in an interview with the author. "You have to take a servant's mentality to know that you are serving in the best interests of the university you represent and to know that the student-athletes are your primary concern in all decisions. You have to understand that it's not about you, it's about them. And it always will be. That's what we are here for—to make sure that we are providing them with the best college experience possible."

DEVELOPING RELATIONSHIPS

Battle expressed what should be the credo for everyone involved in sports finance and administration. The old saying that you should treat others the way you would like to be treated is especially true for those working in this field. The many jobs dealing with economics and finance in every sports business, particularly at the college and professional levels, are often interconnected. The success of one employee can be dependent on the success of a colleague. Developing positive relationships through fair and friendly treatment is the only recipe for achievement.

College and high school athletic directors must be outgoing and visible on their campuses. University of Missouri AD Mike Alden is shown here addressing boosters.

The same is true in outside relationships. Strong communication skills are essential, whether dealing with fans, alumni, media members, advertisers, boosters, or corporate sponsors. The members of each of these groups contribute in one way or another to the revenue needed to run successful high school, college, and professional sports businesses. In the sports industry, just as in life, you will encounter a wide range of personalities and personal and professional motivations. Understanding them is the best way to maximize each professional contact, opportunity, and relationship.

MAKING MONEY

The number of jobs in finance and administration increases at each higher level of team sports, as does the amount of money in play. The athletic director is responsible for every aspect of fund income and distribution in high school sports. Among the most successful in Ohio is Jeff Cassella, who is athletic director at Mentor High School in the northeast suburbs of Cleveland.

Mentor is the most populous high school in the state and a regular state championship contender in several sports. The Mentor Cardinals boys basketball team won the 2013 Division I state title. Mentor teams that have advanced deep into postseason play brought in money through ticket sales and promotions. This revenue was spurred not only by the success on the field or court, but also through the work of Cassella, as well as his colleagues, community members, and students.

Cassella even hopes for luck from Mother Nature. "I am in charge of the entire budget for my department," he explained in an interview with the author. "Most high school athletic departments are self-sufficient. Therefore, gate receipts and expenses have to be carefully monitored. You must be a good communicator to be able to help the department raise funds through fund-raising efforts and booster groups...In Ohio, football is the biggest moneymaker, so you hope for good weather on Friday nights and having a competitive team that your community can support. I would suggest getting as many students involved as possible, as it drives the community to become more involved."

SPORTS FINANCE: BREAKING IT DOWN

What is true for Cassella's Mentor Cardinals is also true throughout the world of sports business. Winning teams attract fans and create promotional, marketing, and advertising possibilities. But while the athletic director and a comparatively small staff are almost solely involved in the finance and administration of high school and small college programs, the number of contributors grows exponentially at major colleges and on the payrolls of professional sports franchises. Each big college athletic department or pro organization boasts many employees working to bolster the economic well-being of their programs.

One glance at the list of employees dealing in economics in prominent university athletic departments or professional sports franchises makes one appreciate the teamwork necessary to conduct financial business. For instance, Battle heads a vast athletic department at the University of Alabama, with eight separate branches working in the financial arena. The following gives an idea of the number of employees responsible for the economic well-being of a major college athletic department:

- Battle works closely with the chief financial officer, but one of his associate athletic directors is designated as a business specialist.

- The Tide Pride department features a manager of fiscal affairs.

- The business office boasts eight employees, including two holding the title of manager of business affairs.

- Several compliance officers serve in the economic realm by ensuring that the athletic department remains in line with National Collegiate Athletic Association (NCAA) standards regarding scholarships and other aspects of running the program within the rules.

- The Crimson Tide Foundation features several employees who work with boosters and others to attract donors and gifts to the athletic department.

- The Crimson Tide Sports Marketing department employs a corporate sponsorship coordinator and several account executives.

- The Promotions and Trademark Licensing department boasts a staff of six, including three directors with various duties and two assistant directors.

The sale of sports-related merchandise is an important money-making tool for college athletic departments. Such merchandise is shown here at a University of Alabama bookstore.

- The ticket office features six employees, including a director of tickets who also serves as an assistant athletic director.

Though the University of Alabama stands out as having one of the most successful athletic departments in the country and has established perhaps the greatest football program in the United States, its number of employees dealing with economic and financial issues is not at all unusual or atypical in the world of major college sports.

The job description of some professionals working in college sports administration falls less in the economic realm. Some focus on the maintenance and management of facilities such as football stadiums, basketball arenas, and even tennis courts and golf courses, but funds for any upkeep and renovations must be approved. Those in student services seek to ensure that the school is serving the best interests of the athletes. Others work as liaisons between the athletic and educational departments to maximize the athletes' academic potential. Also included among college sports administrators are sports information directors (SID) and media relations specialists, each of whom serves the interests and needs of the print, television, radio, and online media. Yet even those employees work within a budget and must address financial restrictions.

Bill Battle makes certain that all employees are aware of their obligations to the overall economic health of the department. "Staying under budget for all of our individual sports programs, developing new revenue streams and fund-raising techniques, and dealing with the ever-demanding challenge of maintaining, developing, and enhancing facilities are all financial aspects of running a major college athletic program," Battle said. "All of those things are a constant in athletics management these days. Fiscal responsibility involves so much more than just being a responsible steward of your current budget. It's challenging, but it's one of the most vitally important aspects of the job."

THE PRO GAME

Fiscal responsibility is one of the most vitally important aspects of the job for those who work in professional sports organizations. In professional team sports, all economic responsibilities trickle down from the owner. In addition, each franchise answers to the standards enforced by the leagues in which they reside, unlike college athletic programs that are subject to the governing authority of the National Collegiate Athletic Association.

The rules that govern professional leagues, as well as the wealth and spending decisions made by team owners, determine the individual budgets of professional franchises and teams. The owners decide how revenue is distributed throughout the league and shared, to varying

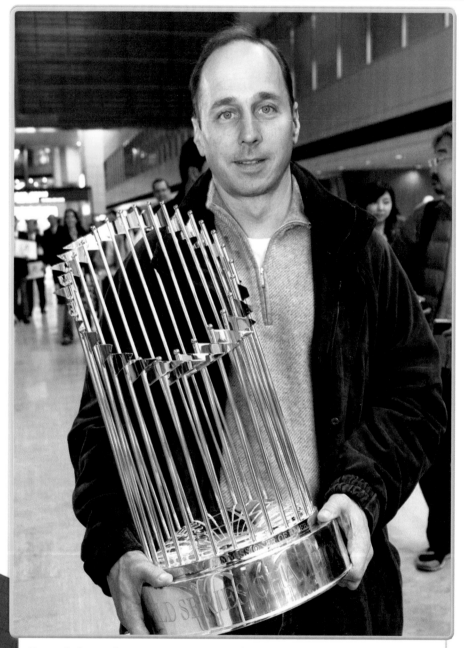

The goal of any college sports program or professional franchise is to win championships. New York Yankees general manager Brian Cashman is seen here holding the 2011 World Series trophy.

extents, by the member teams. In the National Football League (NFL), National Basketball Association (NBA), and National Hockey League (NHL), salary caps restrict the money owners and their teams are allowed to set aside for player salaries. Major League Baseball (MLB) owners are free to spend as much or as little money on player payroll as they wish. This policy has created an imbalance between the richest and poorest teams on the field and has resulted in criticism of baseball's system.

Professional sports franchises boast a different business model than that of college athletic departments. They must earn more money to fund the huge player payrolls of the modern era. The highest-spending Major League Baseball teams, for instance, sometimes pay their players as much as $200 million a year. But television and radio deals earn professional teams and leagues billions of dollars. The hugely popular NFL has attracted particularly lucrative television contracts. Media relations departments also play a role in the economic health of pro teams in that they cater to newspapers and electronic media outlets that provide advertising and publicity, which in turn attract fans.

PROMOTIONS, SALES, AND MARKETING

The growth in job opportunities among professional franchises has been staggering. One example was cited by

$PORTS AND SALARIES

Salary caps and free agency are two huge factors in maintaining competitive balance in baseball, football, and basketball. Here is a look at the relevant rules in each of those sports:

Major League Baseball

Salary cap: This league has no salary cap. Teams are free to spend as much or little as they wish on player salaries. But MLB has implemented a luxury tax on teams that spend more than $178 million in salaries. A penalty of 22.5 percent for first-time "offenders" and 50 percent for teams that exceed the limit in three separate seasons is paid to the league and then distributed into an MLB growth fund.

Free agency: A player remains the property of a team for six seasons unless he is released from his contract. He can then become a free agent.

National Football League

Salary cap: The NFL salary cap was raised to $120 million in 2011. A salary floor was instituted in 2013 that demanded that each team spend at least 88.8 percent of the cap over two four-year periods.

Free agency: NFL players who have played in at least six regular-season games in three accrued seasons are restricted free agents. They can sign with another team, but their previous team can keep them if they match the offer. Players with four such years of experience become unrestricted free agents.

National Basketball Association

Salary cap: The NBA instituted a salary cap of $58.04 million in December 2011. It is a "soft" cap, however, meaning that teams are allowed to exceed it to retain the rights to a player already on the team. The league also has a salary floor, but teams are not penalized if their player payroll dips below the floor by the end of each season. The salary cap is much lower than in the NFL and MLB, but it must be remembered that the rosters are much smaller.

Free agency: NBA players become restricted free agents after four seasons unless they have been released from their contracts. They are unrestricted free agents after five seasons.

University of Massachusetts sports management professor Glenn M. Wong in his 2013 book, *The Comprehensive Guide to Careers in Sports.* Wong wrote that the NBA Boston Celtics featured a business staff of seven employees in the early 1980s. Within thirty years, that number had grown to more than seventy.

That employment explosion can be explained in part by the use of aggressive promotion and marketing techniques to spur ticket sales, advertising revenue, and merchandising of the team brand. Sports franchises spend their own money on advertising to lure fans and work

Corporate sponsorship is a key component to financing such professional sports as tennis, which features superstars such as Spaniard Rafael Nadal. Nadal is in action here at the U.S. Open, which enjoys the sponsorship of Merecedes-Benz, whose logo appears on the net.

with businesses that believe they can sell more of their products if they are affiliated with a popular local professional franchise.

Among those working to develop corporate sponsorships for the NFL's Denver Broncos is Brady Kellogg, who serves as vice president of corporate partnerships. "Corporate partnerships are when a company enters into an agreement with the Denver Broncos to leverage the Broncos' brand and assets to help promote their business," Kellogg explained in an interview with the author. "The goal is different for each partner, whether selling cars, opening checking accounts, driving traffic to restaurants, or whatever. Offering our assets to help drive financial or other benefits for the partner, the Broncos are compensated for their role in this process…[A]longside TV revenue, ticket sales, and merchandising, corporate partnerships represent an important source of revenue to the organization. In addition, corporate partners play a key role in extending the visibility of the Broncos brand. Partners frequently use our name, logo, or brand in their packaging and advertising, whether billboards, TV, print, or whatever. Fans often benefit from special giveaways or promotional offers funded by corporate partners."

FARTHER AFIELD

Corporate partnerships are also critical to the success of professional and amateur sports organizations that receive less attention. The U.S. Tennis Association (USTA), Professional Golfers Association of America (PGA), USA Hockey, U.S. Soccer Federation (USSF), and USA Gymnastics serve as the national governing boards for their individual sports. Their payrolls include employees who work in marketing, promotion, and finance both at the national and local levels.

These organizations and other smaller groups that promote specific sports must not only work within strict budgets, but they must also attract revenue through more creative means. Their counterparts in the world of major college and professional leagues such as the NFL, NBA, and Major League Baseball earn billions of dollars through advertising, ticket and merchandise sales, and the selling of broadcast rights. Individual professional sports such as golf and tennis lure paying customers as well, though these are comparatively few in number. But organizations that run amateur adult and youth sports such as gymnastics and hockey rely upon the selling of memberships to participants of those activities and their families. People hired in the finance and administration departments of such amateur sports organizations use promotion, marketing, and sales techniques to convince those who embrace their sport to join as members, and these memberships give them certain benefits.

Even the most obscure and niche-oriented sports are governed by organizations that employ finance and administration specialists. Organizations such as USA Table Tennis, U.S. Squash, USA Badminton, and dozens of others promote sports embraced by comparatively few people. But they give many who love them an opportunity to work on behalf of a sport about which they feel passionate. And passion is what everyone yearns to feel about their job.

Chapter 2
PLANTING THE SEEDS FOR SUCCESS

It is never too early to begin thinking about and preparing for a career. That certainly holds true for those considering a future in sports finance and administration. Most promising about such a career is that it features a wide range of opportunities. Dozens of positions fall under the sports finance and administration umbrella, including those at the youth, prep, college, and professional levels, working for athletic teams, facilities, events, or organizations. High school students with either vague or crystal-clear notions about a desire to pursue such a career have plenty of time to zero in on the specific career they wish to pursue within the broader field of sports finance and administration.

A love for sports is often the strongest inspiration for an eventual career choice. Only a small percentage of high school athletes who participate on sports teams prove talented enough to play at the college level, particularly at a major Division I school. And only a very small number of those few gifted athletes emerge to compete professionally. So it must be understood at an early age that while a drive to maximize athletic potential is admirable, a career in sports does not have to be limited to playing. Learning various aspects of sports finance and administration in high school often proves to be a valuable tool for forging an eventual career in the field.

LEARNING INSIDE AND OUTSIDE THE CLASSROOM

The important first step on the path to that career is making the decision to maximize academic potential. On a daily basis, everyone working in the field of sports finance and administration uses his or her knowledge of a variety of subjects that were acquired in the classroom.

Bill Battle not only used his athletic talent to play football with the Crimson Tide in the early 1960s, but he also combined his academic achievements with his athletic background to thrive as a head coach at the University of Tennessee and as athletic director at the University of Alabama. Battle stresses the importance of a solid academic foundation to those seeking a career in sports finance and administration. "I believe that having been an athlete has made me a better person overall, primarily due to the life lessons I learned by playing team and individual sports at a young age," Battle says. "So, obviously, I think understanding what a student-athlete goes through on the athletic *and* academic side has a tremendously beneficial impact on being an effective coach or administrator. From an academic and overall personal growth standpoint, I would strive to do well academically in all facets, particularly regarding grammar, math, and any business aspects you can get involved in."

Gaining a strong business knowledge from teachers such as the one shown here is critical for college students seeking a career in sports finance and administration.

Each subject that Battle cites provides specific benefits to most sports finance and administration careers. Grammar and other facets of what is learned in English classes are used to communicate well on the job with colleagues and the public. Those who work in marketing, promotions, sales, or communications, as well as athletic directors and sports information directors, must be well-spoken and convincing writers. Anyone who works on the finance side of sports must be proficient in math and business. High school students who do not take those particular subjects seriously will not be able to compete effectively with other job applicants when pursuing a career in this field.

Battle also refers to the advantage that participating in high school athletics gives those contemplating a future in the sports world. One might wonder how experience with athletics would help the vast majority of job applicants for sports finance positions, who are not talented enough to become professional athletes and who do not seek a career in coaching. It must be understood that the best way to gain an appreciation for sports, athletes, and how teams and leagues function as businesses, is to experience competition and learn firsthand what it takes

College students can take many paths to a career in sports finance and administration, but some involvement in sports is important. Shown here are equipment managers at work at the University of South Carolina.

to excel. Having competed or participated (perhaps as team manager, equipment manager, score and records keeper, team fund-raiser, etc.) in athletics is not a requirement for success in most finance and administration jobs. Yet experience with athletic events provides a perspective, vocabulary, and cultural familiarity that will certainly prove helpful in making a mark in the sports industry.

THE SHADOW KNOWS

Those seeking a career in the sports industry as nonathletes can often learn more from attending games than playing in them because they can focus on all the outside influences that go into staging a sporting event and running an athletic program. Jeff Cassella, who serves as the athletic director at Mentor High School in Ohio, encourages students who yearn to get into sports finance and administration to do more than just watch the sports they love or that are the most popular. He advises them to take in games in a variety of sports, even those that typically don't attract the most fans. "I would suggest going to as many games as possible, not just football and basketball," Cassella says. "Watch how things operate. Ask to shadow your high school athletic director. You'll learn that every level has something to offer. How a department runs at a small rural high school is much different than how it runs at a large suburban or urban high school."

Cassella recommends following athletic directors (ADs) in their daily routines and particularly during sporting events. Though ADs understand that sports such as basketball and, especially, football bring in the most revenue and are critical to bolstering the athletic department budget, they cannot ignore the sports most often neglected by fans. Athletic directors are among the most prominent public figures at a school and among the most involved in student, alumni, and public relations. They generally consider it important to be present at even those games that tend to be poorly attended, which includes just about any sport outside football and basketball. ADs realize that

Hiring coaches is a critical job for sports owners and general managers. Seen here in a game against Notre Dame is University of Pittsburgh football coach Dave Wannstedt.

every sport is important, especially to the participating student athletes, regardless of how big a crowd they draw and how much media attention they attract.

Shadowing the athletic director gives students a sense of how to prioritize tasks in a job that is full of them. It provides an opportunity to get a feel for how an athletic director balances many responsibilities, including the scheduling of opponents for all his or her teams, which is particularly challenging at independent schools not affiliated with a league. The AD must work diligently to remain within a strict budget, partner with fund-raisers, and stay on top of the abundant paperwork that sometimes keeps the AD tied to the office. Yet the AD must also remain accessible to coaches, students, athletes, and the public. It is not a nine-to-five job. After all, ADs are obligated—and generally eager—to work events such as football and basketball games, which are most often played at night.

Students with introverted personalities should probably consider more behind-the-scenes work in sports finance and administration. Athletic directors are public relations specialists. They must keep a positive outlook and push to imbue others with a sense of optimism and enthusiasm. A shy athletic director will probably not be up to these tasks. The job also requires a lot of energy. High school athletic directors are on the go constantly. Though they must sometimes work alone in their offices, they do not remain there for long.

DEEP IN THE HEART OF TEXAS

High school football is a popular sport in all states. But it has been described as a religion in Texas. High school–level Texas football was even the subject of the popular television drama *Friday Night Lights*. One of the many examples of the popularity of high school football in Texas is the annual rivalry between Odessa and Permian, two teams featured in *Friday Night Lights*, which draws about thirty thousand fans.

Some believe, however, that the folks in the Dallas suburb of Allen, who in 2009 approved the building of a new football stadium for their high school team, are the ultimate Texas football fans. The cost? Sixty million dollars. One school official admitted that the expenditure will never be fully recouped. And that fact irked writer Doug Mataconis, who offered the following view on the Web site Outside the Beltway:

> This strikes me as just a bit ridiculous. It's bad enough that they spent $60 million, which is larger than the budgets of some school systems in this country, on a football stadium instead of on academics, or on upgrading the school facilities that all the students use. But, they did so knowing that they'd never get that money back. … Making an investment that you know you'll never pay for in the end is monumentally stupid.

Mataconis went on to complain that in a nation in which students lag behind their peers from other countries in standardized tests, such an expenditure is "ridiculous." He offered that the voters of Allen should be ashamed of themselves and ask if the stadium is more important than the future of their children.

Cassella advises high school athletes and nonathletes who are considering a career as an athletic director to keep a keen eye on the coaches of various sports working in their high schools. Most students are not trained to evaluate job performance at a professional level. But they can gain an understanding of why some coaches are more successful than others as tacticians, motivators, and developers of good team dynamics. It is never too early for a prospective athletic director to develop an ability to judge coaching. Even though so much of the job revolves around budgetary concerns, evaluation of coaches is also an important part of an AD's job description.

MOTIVATION AND CURIOSITY

Motivation is the key element for high school students who yearn to forge a career in sports finance and administration. One must be motivated to soak up and study what is provided in math and business classes, both of which are critical to success in the field. One must be motivated to discover learning opportunities—including volunteer work and internships—at local colleges or in athletic organizations. One must be motivated to gain pertinent knowledge from athletic directors, coaches, and players, often by asking them for informational interviews and observing them at work. One must be motivated to attend high school, college, and professional sporting events in

Coaches and athletic directors should remain close. University of Nebraska AD Bo Pelini (*left*) and coach Tom Osborne are shown here leading their team on the field before a football game.

order to study all the key elements to which administrators contribute—from facility preparation, advertising, promotion, and marketing to the hiring of officials and the offering of scholarships and multimillion-dollar contracts. Prospective sports administrators should take a different, more critical view of the events and surroundings at a sporting event than would an ordinary fan in order to evaluate how effectively money is being spent and earned by the team or organization.

Young people considering a career in sports finance and administration should not be afraid to inquire about anything involving the business. One advantage for high school athletes seeking such a career is that they are in the best position to learn about the all-encompassing job of athletic director. Cassella believes his job description calls for him to communicate often with his athletes and coaches. "Students who would like to know what I do should watch, observe, and ask questions," Cassella says. "Any good athletic director is around the teams often. Whether that is at practice or games, they should be really visible. If they are not, they are not doing the job that they should be. I make it a point to go to practices and talk to the athletes as much as possible."

That is where shyness becomes a liability. Some high school students are simply too reluctant to approach athletic directors with a series of questions about their job responsibilities. Shedding that fear and putting yourself out there will not only result in greater knowledge, but also a sense of comfort and security in personal communications that is critical to any job in the field. Even those who do not work with the public must possess good communication skills with colleagues, so it is wise to get as much practice as possible meeting and greeting in high school. One must also realize that most athletic directors would be flattered to field questions about their jobs. They will most likely be quite willing to put in the time and energy to help out a young person interested in pursuing a career in the sports finance and administration field.

The AD would certainly suggest that one critical step toward achieving one's professional goals is finding a college that offers sports finance and administration as a major and has had a successful history of teaching it and placing its graduates in good jobs within the field. It is never too early to start researching college programs. It is at the university of your choice where your career really begins.

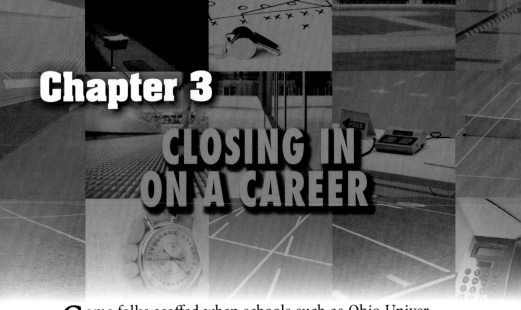

Chapter 3

CLOSING IN ON A CAREER

S ome folks scoffed when schools such as Ohio University and the University of Massachusetts launched the first sports business management programs in the nation in the 1970s. They joked that all it would teach is how to

Ohio University boasted one of the first sports administration programs of any college in the country. Holding the football here is program alumnus Basil DeVito, who went on to become a high-ranking executive for World Wrestling Entertainment (WWE) and the XFL.

mix Gatorade. The colleges and students have had the last laugh, however. Such programs have educated many students and resulted in thousands of highly qualified and professional individuals forging careers in sports finance and administration.

But some people, even those preparing to earn a master's degree in the field, still misunderstand what that training will entail. They unrealistically envision a more glamorous side of sports. Jim Riordan, director of the masters of business administration in sports management program at Florida Atlantic University, feels obligated to burst their bubble. "People think they're going to sit around all day and watch [New York Yankees shortstop] Derek Jeter take batting practice or [NFL quarterback] Rex Grossman throw touchdown passes," Riordan explained to Menachem Wecker of *U.S. News & World Report*. "And when you say to them, 'OK, let's look at a business plan … or let's do due diligence on a potential team sale or team evaluation,' they look at you like you have three heads. My biggest challenge in accepting students today is separating the sports fan from the sports business student."

IT'S NO GAME: THE BUSINESS OF SPORTS

If graduate students have the wrong impression of what studying sports finance and administration really entails, one can only imagine how many students entering college misunderstand what the major is all about. They learn quickly that while they are free to enjoy watching the sports teams at their schools and become involved in their athletic programs behind the scenes, learning about sports business in the classroom can be less exciting than soaking in the action. They discover that finance and administration are essential aspects of the sports world, but they can be a bit dry compared to watching a wide receiver sprint downfield and catch an over-the-shoulder pass in-stride for a touchdown.

Yet the sports finance and administration field is wide-ranging enough to allow students to gear themselves toward whatever most closely suits their personalities and interests. The Web site that details undergraduate sports management studies at Ohio University gives the following explanation of the various career possibilities for its students:

Job functions in the sport industry include facility management, sport promotion and marketing, sport media, customer or community relations, sport sponsorship, licensing, sport information, and sport law. Common job titles include marketing and promotions director, academic services for student athletics, corporate sales director, director of ticketing and finance, sporting goods sales representative, facility coordinator, athletic director, compliance director, athletic business manager, fitness manager, and program director of community sport programs.

Sports management is a comparatively new field of study in American universities. It began with Ohio University and the University of Massachusetts in the 1970s and has since been adopted by more than three hundred schools. Programs are now also available in Europe and Africa, as well as such countries as Australia, New Zealand, and India.

The programs at various universities throughout the United States delve deeply into the financial realm, which is generally considered the domain of sports administration. Sports administration programs also teach aspects of the sports industry that fall into what is perceived as management. The line between the definitions of sports management and sports administration is certainly blurred—even at the upper academic level. Some offer the former as an undergraduate major and the latter only for graduate students. Others boast undergraduate degrees in sports administration. Still others combine the two in a sports management/administration major. But in schools that do not distinguish between the two, the course requirements for each can be nearly identical.

What is most important to understand is that colleges around the country have considered sports management and administration burgeoning industries and worthy of their attention for the last forty years. Among them is Northwestern University in Illinois, which offers a master of arts in sports administration. Its Web site explains why it provides such a course of study. It points out that only a tiny number of people blossom into professional athletes, coaches, or top executives. Sports marketing and administration jobs are expected to continue to grow, however, because of demographics and an increased demand for "sophisticated organizations" that specialize in youth sports. Indeed, according to the Bureau of Labor Statistics,

There are a variety of jobs that fall under the category of sports administration. Shown here is New York Yankees director of stadium tours Tony Morante (*right*) giving a tour of Yankee Stadium.

sports-related jobs are expected to increase 23 percent for the decade ending in 2018, a much larger increase than the average for other employment sectors.

WHAT IS A COMPLIANCE OFFICER?

The NCAA does not have a soft heart when it comes to punishing athletic programs that break its rules. Those who knowingly or unknowingly violate the rules regarding recruiting, the amateur status of athletes, or any other NCAA laws have been subject to severe penalties, including bans from postseason bowl games and the loss of scholarships.

That is why many athletic departments have hired compliance officers. It is their job not only to fully understand every nuance of NCAA (and conference) rules, but also to make sure that every athletic director, coach, and athlete is aware of them as well. It has become one of the least publicized but most important jobs in any athletic department. In July 2013, University of Miami head coach Al Golden told the cable sports news network ESPN that compliance officers should be mandatory in every college athletic program. He added that, among other things, it would keep athletes on the straight and narrow.

Compliance officers do not merely help enforce NCAA rules. They also work to keep athletes, many of whom come from poor socioeconomic backgrounds, out of trouble and far from the temptation to cash in illegally on their celebrity. University of North

Carolina director of compliance Amy Herman told the South Florida *Sun-Sentinel*, "We don't expect them [student athletes] to know all the rules because we don't know all the rules, and we deal with it on a daily basis. What we expect of them is that they know enough of the rules to know when to ask. If they have a question about something or if something raises even a tiny red flag, they know to pick up the phone and make the call to us."

Even the most cursory glance at the course offerings for students in the Ohio University sports administration program—and others across the American college landscape—gives an idea of how many options are available for students to find a niche in sports finance and administration. Those with more outgoing personalities might be more likely to choose a career in marketing, promotions, sales, media relations, or as a director of an athletic department or community sports program. Those who prefer to work behind the scenes might be better suited to a job as an accountant, facilities coordinator, financial officer, or business manager. But students who enter college sports administration programs receive an all-encompassing education that allows them to take their time to decide on a specific career direction.

Volunteering is a great first step for those seeking a career in sports finance and administration. Shown here is a volunteer handing out cups of water at the New York City Marathon.

INTERNSHIPS

One experience that speeds up that decision-making process is an internship. Finding organizations or leagues that offer internships to college students takes research, and landing one requires time and effort, but the benefits cannot be underestimated. Professional leagues, teams, media outlets, and college athletic departments all seek interns from sports business programs. School counselors encourage students to volunteer with athletic organizations or for athletic events. This gives candidates valuable hands-on experience in the industry and allows them to apply the knowledge they learned in the classroom. It also increases their opportunities for future employment. Internships give students a better understanding about the area to which they are best suited within the world of sports finance and administration. They also allow students to forge professional relationships that can be helpful upon graduation, during a job search, and in the early years of employment and career building.

Internships, however, must be earned through strong work in the classroom. Many schools require students to maintain at least a 3.5 grade point average to be considered for an internship. After all, a college sports administration program yearns to sustain its relationships with sports organizations, so its practice is to recommend only its most promising and most accomplished students for internships. Qualified students are usually offered internships in their final year of undergraduate studies, and they earn credits toward graduation.

Another avenue for internships is the Internet. Job sites such as Internships.com and JobsInSports.com can prove beneficial, but competition is fierce. Internships with a professional sports team, particularly those in the NBA, NFL, NHL, and MLB, are highly sought after and receive many thousands of applications for every available position. The MLB Cleveland Indians recently received 1,500 applications for six available internships, according to the team human resources specialist (as reported in *The Comprehensive Guide to Careers in Sports*).

Larger universities with expansive athletic programs that offer a wide array of sports are more likely to feature internship programs within their athletic departments. A glance at the 2013 athletic department staff directory for Ohio State, which boasts one of the most extensive sports programs in the nation, reveals that interns are used in several areas that fall within the financial realm, including compliance, event management, promotions, communications, merchandising, and ticket office.

Gaining an internship with a college athletic program or professional franchise can be an important step to a career. This young intern is selling game tickets at the University of Tennessee.

Such internships are particularly valuable for those seeking a career in a college setting. They provide experience in the same line of work that could be made available to students once they graduate. Athletic department internships are also a proving ground. During them, successful students may convince the athletic director to make them full-time employees or motivate the AD to strongly recommend them for jobs at other schools. And making a strong impression on colleagues who are established in a college athletic department can have a positive impact on one's career. The old adage "It's not what you know, but who you know" is not completely accurate because a strong knowledge base is critical to success. But impressing those with contacts in the sports finance and administration world can certainly prove beneficial.

SUMMER PROGRAMS

Summer programs and Internet sites that list internship and training opportunities abound for high school students seeking to explore a career in sports administration and management. For example, Georgetown University in Washington, D.C., is home to a sports industry management program, which allows students to live on campus while studying the finer points of sports administration. Tuition includes housing and all meals. During the course of the program, students gain knowledge of sports administration through lectures from Georgetown faculty and visiting experts in the field, tours of sports facilities, and meetings with sports franchise executives. The wide-ranging topics covered include ethics, leadership, marketing, media, communication, sales, promotions, community relations, finance, contract negotiations, and facility management.

Those seeking a career centered on sports finance might be more interested in a program at the University of Pennsylvania's Wharton Sports Business Academy. The summer program for high school juniors and seniors

Hundreds of American colleges offer classes in sports finance and administration. One such class is in session here.

provides an all-encompassing learning experience about sports finance, including courses in sports management, law, negotiation, marketing, and leadership. The program also provides an overview of the business and legal aspects of a variety of college, Olympic, and professional sports businesses. The Academy's Web site states:

> WSBA students will learn about ownership, sports agents, and celebrity endorsements as they meet with leaders in the sports business world. Students will visit some of the region's most important sports facilities, and ultimately gain insight into the leadership, management, and increasingly global nature of sports business. Through academic and co-curricular activities, WSBA students will have the opportunity to test their potential as future sports business leaders.

BOOK LEARNING AND LIFE LEARNING

Though internships can help students find employment upon graduation, they are not a requirement when applying for jobs. Majoring in sports administration or management is certainly the smoothest, surest pathway to success in the field. It also prepares students for a wide array of sports finance and administration jobs in extremely interesting and dynamic athletic organizations. *Bloomberg BusinessWeek* magazine tracked eight sports management majors who have graduated since 2001. One worked as an intern at the 2008 Summer Olympics in China. Another served with the Sports Philanthropy Project to advise professional athletes on how to make a positive impact on local communities. Another was employed by the Massachusetts Special Olympics, an annual event for the physically challenged. Yet another worked as a fund-raiser for the NHL's Washington Capitals.

The common denominator is that each of these individuals earned sports management degrees in college. There is debate among professionals in the sports finance and administration field about the best course of action for career seekers. Some feel it is prudent for students to major in sports management at the undergraduate level only. Others believe one should work toward an undergraduate and master's degree in the field. Still others downplay the importance of an undergraduate degree in sports management or administration but believe career seekers should definitely pursue a master's in it. University of Alabama athletic director Bill Battle offers the following view regarding those seeking to follow in his footsteps: "Obviously, some business training would be valuable, but I don't think it matters as much at the undergraduate level," he says. "But at the graduate level is where some focus in the business administration, sports management, or other specific fields might be most beneficial."

Denver Broncos director of corporate partnerships Brady Kellogg expresses his view that everyone should forge a career in the area he or she feels most comfortable in, based on his or her background and what line of work is being pursued. But Kellogg also emphasizes the importance of hands-on experience. "Our staff [with the Broncos] is comprised of individuals from a variety of backgrounds, each of whom provides a different perspective, so it is tough to recommend one particular course of preparation," Kellogg says. "Relevant job experience is certainly a plus, whether that is working in relevant jobs while in high school or college with their [school] teams, local professional teams, or even companies or media partners working with teams."

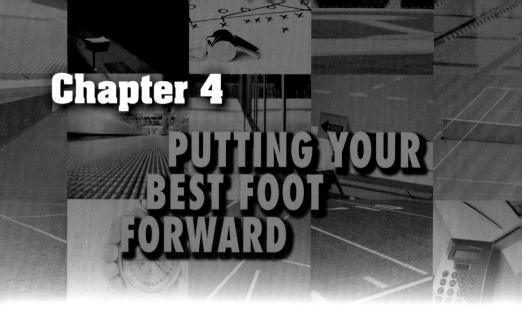

Chapter 4

PUTTING YOUR BEST FOOT FORWARD

Perhaps former University of Texas football coach Darrell Royal expressed best what should be the motto for graduates looking to catch a break and a good job out of college. He has said that luck is what happens when preparation meets opportunity. Employers in the sports finance and administration industry are flooded with résumés from recent college graduates. They receive hundreds, sometimes thousands, of inquiries for a few openings. Only the most impressive candidates are selected for interviews. And only one of them is chosen for each job.

Every step in the process of landing work in the business can be painstaking. But there is no shortcut. One must do both soul searching and exhaustive homework to achieve success. Understanding what job best suits your background and passion will allow you to target a particular area in the field.

Before the advent of personal computers, e-mail, and the Internet, college graduates were forced to research job

Like many recent college graduates, those looking for work in sports finance and administration typically struggle to find entry-level jobs. These young people are seeking employment in Florida.

opportunities at the library, type cover letters and résumés on a typewriter, make copies at an office store, and send them out by snail mail. The modern graduate can do all his or her work from the comfort of home, sending and receiving documents and correspondence instantaneously. But he or she still must be thorough and detail-oriented.

RÉSUMÉS AND NETWORKING

The first step is to seek out job possibilities in your area of expertise and interest. One can subscribe to such publications as *Street and Smith's SportsBusiness Journal* and scour job Web sites such as TeamWorkOnline.com and WorkInSports.com for openings. The importance of your work history in college also comes into play at this stage. Sports finance and administration professionals you might have impressed in an internship or summer job often have knowledge of openings in the field. So might counselors or older friends from your college sports management program. Do not hesitate to ask them to keep you posted and provide personal references and recommendations to prospective employers.

The next step is to create a résumé that highlights your academic and professional achievements. Even the best students will strike out with a résumé that only accentuates a strong grade point average in high school and college. A clean, error-free, one-page résumé that emphasizes not only academic strength but also relevant work experience and extracurricular activities in high school and college is far more impressive. A separate page of complimentary quotes about you from college administrators or work colleagues is also a plus. Do not use friends or family members as references unless they are employed in the industry.

It is wise to maximize any relationships that could help you land your first job. Consult with any acquaintances who work in the industry. Think about former classmates or teachers with contacts. Learn about possible career placement programs featured at your high school or college. What about coaches or athletic directors with

The importance of writing well cannot be understated for those eyeing a career in sports administration. This student from Syracuse, New York, is going over his English paper with an instructor.

whom you were once associated? Most people are glad to help because it makes them feel good about themselves.

Perhaps you are aware of events frequented or run by sports industry executives during which you can make direct contacts. This is called networking, and it can make the difference between unemployment and a promising start to a career in sports finance and administration. In *The Comprehensive Guide to Careers in Sports*, one community relations coordinator for an NFL franchise recommends gathering up the courage to "cold call" higher-ups in an organization that interest you. Ask for an informational interview or the opportunity to shadow them at work for a period of time. He urges career seekers to, "Get out and meet people face to face. Paper résumés are worthless in this industry. People only hire individuals whom they know, so the best thing to do is call people up and ask them if they have time to talk in person. Either ask if you can do a personal interview at the office, shadow them for a day, or offer to buy them lunch. Whatever you can do to make yourself memorable is important."

Nevertheless, a résumé is necessary because it is impossible to make personal contact with every person in a position to hire. It is important to blanket with résumés all employers who interest you and for whom you would like to work. But there is no doubt that an aggressive approach to meeting as many people in charge of hiring as possible is far better than merely sending out résumés and not making personal contact with influential decision makers. There is no substitute for hustle, which displays a sense of confidence and desire that cannot be matched by an e-mail correspondence. One should at least follow up each e-mailed résumé with a phone call and provide a copy of the résumé at every face-to-face meeting.

Sports organizations, particularly the NFL, NBA, NHL, and MLB franchises, receive overwhelming responses to job openings, even in the finance and administration realm. Anything a young prospect can do to stand out in a positive manner is a plus. Proving your passion and talent through action will make a far greater impact on an employer than even the most impressive résumé.

PARLAYING VOLUNTEER GIGS AND INTERNSHIPS INTO A PAYING JOB

Once you are armed with a college degree, impressive résumé, and strong references, it is time to seek out your first job. But keep in mind that the résumé and references can always be strengthened through actual work experience. It is never too late for recent college graduates seeking a full-time job to burnish their résumé through volunteering or unpaid internships.

Volunteers in the world of sports can perform any number of jobs. One such volunteer is seen here displaying scores at a professional golf tournament held in Alabama.

Organizers of sporting events such as golf and tennis tournaments or marathons are often looking for volunteers. So are youth baseball, softball, and soccer leagues. Helping in whatever capacity required by such organizations is greatly appreciated and can demonstrate to potential employers your work ethic, can-do spirit, and passion for the industry. Let the leaders in such leagues and organizations know that you have graduated with a degree in business, sports administration, or sports management. They might be impressed enough to provide a paying job at the end of your volunteer or internship gig.

Who knows? Maybe you will enjoy the volunteer job or internship and your colleagues enough to seek permanent employment and launch your career with that organization. If you perform well enough as a volunteer or unpaid intern, a paid position could be in your future.

BE WILLING TO RELOCATE AND START AT THE BOTTOM

It is advisable for graduates focusing on a career in sports finance and administration, particularly those living in small towns or rural areas, to be open to relocation. This does not necessarily mean moving to a major metropolitan area. Minor league baseball and basketball teams, high school and college athletic departments, and many sports-related organizations often make their homes outside the major cities. But a willingness to move anywhere in the country not only provides a chance to launch your career, but it also opens the door to exciting new experiences, new working relationships, and new friends and professional contacts in a new community. Those willing to relocate for a good job offer are most likely to find work that allows them to use their advanced finance and administration skills immediately.

What the college graduate should realize, however, is that dreams must be tempered by reality. One should never lose sight of one's ultimate professional goal, but one must also remain patient and realistic. Many people find their first jobs in sports finance and administration disappointing. According to Glenn M. Wong, author of *The Comprehensive Guide to Careers in Sports* and professor of sports management at the University of Massachusetts, recent college graduates should figure on at least two years of toiling at the lowest rung of a business. But at least they have their foot in the door. Wong offers the following perspective and reality check: "There are plenty of presidents/CEOs who started in the mailroom or in fan relationship management (telemarketing or inside sales), but initially wanted a marketing position or a PR position. However, when they took that entry-level job, they committed to being the best mailroom person or the best sales representative that organization ever had."

SKYROCKETING SALARIES

Professional athletes were legally tied to their teams until the 1970s. There was no such thing as free agency unless a franchise voluntarily freed a player from his contract. The result was salaries that paled in comparison to those of today.

A prime example is provided by Major League Baseball. In 1967, a year before the league and the players negotiated their first contract, the minimum salary for players was a mere $6,000 a year. The union battled to win the right to free agency, but the league argued that sports was different than the rest of society, and that if every player could work wherever he wanted at any time, the structure of the sport would crumble. The same model held true in other major professional sports leagues.

A series of compromises was eventually reached, though not without strikes, work stoppages, and other legal battles. The result was that each major professional sports league was forced to grant players free agency after several years of service. The teams' bottom lines skyrocketed. Player salaries jumped in the 1970s and have continued to rise. According to the Major League Baseball Players Association, the average annual salary for players in 1980 was $143,756. It increased to $597,537 in 1990, and $1,895,630 in 2000. By 2012, it had reached $3.2 million.

The NFL has experienced a similar rise from a $23,000 average annual salary in 1970 to $1.9 million in 2010. The average NBA salary was the highest of all by 2013, at $5.2 million. It must be remembered, however, that teams in that league have just fifteen players on their rosters, compared to twenty-five in Major League Baseball and fifty-three in the National Football League.

THE INTERVIEW PROCESS

The euphoric feeling experienced by young people when contacted for a job interview is often tempered by the reality of the situation, especially if it is for a highly sought-after position. Many recent college graduates are unsure about how to best impress those making hiring decisions. Uncertainty and nervousness are two major obstacles that must be overcome. After all, you will likely never get another chance at what could be a wonderful employment opportunity.

Media relations employees piece together media guides every year that provide complete information about players and coaches. They are also valuable sources of organizational information that are highly useful for job applicants.

The most important consideration is to learn everything you can about the organization doing the hiring and what the particular finance and administration job being filled entails. That means poring over the organization's Web site to learn about the history and purpose of the company and, during the interview, asking questions of the employer if there is anything of note that you have not discovered through research. All major sports franchises produce annual media guides that provide job candidates a thorough knowledge of the organization from the front office on down. But it is not always easy to gain the necessary insight about finance-related jobs through media guides or organization Web sites. The best solution is to ask questions about the specific skills the interviewer is seeking. Keep in mind that knowledge is the best antidote to nervousness because it creates a feeling of confidence that you will not stumble over a question. Gaining knowledge before and during the interview is a wise strategy. The interviewer will be impressed by the fact that you have studied his or her organization and the specifics of the job and are asking intelligent and insightful follow-up questions to gain further insight.

Confidence is critical—and it is important to let yours show. As a college graduate, perhaps with a sports administration or sports business degree, you have gained worthy credentials for the job you are seeking. Before your interview, consider how what you learned in school relates to the job description. Learn exactly what skills and duties the job entails and tailor your answers to the interviewer's questions in a way that highlights your relevant education and work experience Ask yourself the following question: What knowledge and skills acquired through my education and previous work experience will convince the interviewer that I am the best candidate for this particular job?

You will likely be asked for a concluding statement at the end of the interview. The best reply is a simple expression of desire to land the job and to work in that particular organization, along with a brief synopsis of why you believe you are an ideal candidate. Sports finance and administration jobs, particularly those offered to recent college graduates, do not place employees in the limelight. They are most often behind the scenes, working anonymously deep within the organization's hierarchy. An expression of willingness to simply perform a job well, without fanfare, is greatly appreciated by those doing the hiring.

That appreciation will grow when you send a thank-you note to the employer for taking the time to discuss the open position with you and for considering your application. Jobs in sports administration are difficult to land. Any polite expression of appreciation and gratitude can help you stand out from the other candidates.

Chapter 5

CAREERS AT THE COLLEGE AND PRO LEVELS

There are so many jobs in sports finance and administration in the United States alone that they cannot all be detailed here. Let us separate how and where those in the business are employed into four levels—professional sports, college sports, high school/middle school sports, and youth/amateur sports. This chapter will focus on the first two, and the following chapter will address the latter two.

WORKING IN THE BIG LEAGUES

The four major professional sports leagues are Major League Baseball (MLB), the National Football League (NFL), the National Basketball Association (NBA), and the National Hockey League (NHL). Also competing for attention are the wide array of minor leagues in baseball and hockey, as well as Major League Soccer (MLS), Major League Lacrosse (MLL), the Arena Football League (AFL), and other smaller professional leagues that feature less popular sports, such as World Team Tennis (WTT).

Internships and jobs in finance and administration with Major League Baseball franchises are tough to land for recent graduates. A first step is to know who is hiring, and what type of candidates they are looking for.

Each of these professional leagues boasts many employees whose work falls under the category of sports finance and administration. The NBA, for instance, lists the following finance and administration categories on its Career Opportunities site (http://careers.peopleclick.com/careerscp/client_nba/external/search.do):

- Business development
- Business management

- Communications
- Community relations
- Event management
- Event planning
- Facilities and management
- Finance
- Marketing partnership
- Marketing/advertising
- Merchandising
- Sales

A recent review of the NBA job site noted fifty-nine job openings within the realm of finance and administration. That league, in particular, has sought to globalize its popularity, resulting in job openings in China, Turkey, India, England, Brazil, and Canada. The NFL has been thwarted in its attempt to gain acceptance across the ocean—NFL Europe featured teams in countries such as Spain, Germany, and England from 1991 to 2007 before folding. The league has since centered its attention on playing occasional regular-season games in Europe and Mexico City, all of which have drawn large crowds. As many as three NFL games a year are now being played in England, where there are an estimated twelve million

American football fans, a huge increase within only a few years.

BEING A TEAM PLAYER

Though it is admirable to set one's sights on a job within the corporate office of a major sports league, a more realistic possibility, particularly for recent college graduates, is to gain employment with an individual team within a league. The major professional athletic leagues have undergone drastic expansion since the 1970s that has doubled, tripled, or even quadrupled their number of teams. One prominent example is the NHL, which has raised its franchise total from six in 1967 to thirty in 2013. Though expansion has slowed markedly since the 1980s, each league has more teams than ever, resulting in a peak number of finance and administration jobs.

The categories of such jobs are virtually the same for every team in every professional league. The Baltimore Orioles, for instance, list in their staff directory six different departments staffed by employees who work directly in the financial realm. Those departments and some of the more prominent individual jobs related to sports finance are listed below:

- Executive management (vice president of business operations)

- Business/administration (chief financial officer, business operations)

- Administration (accounting assistant)

- Finance (vice president, manager, senior accountant, financial analyst, ticket office accountant, accounts receivable manager, payroll manager, accounts payable manager)

- Corporate sales and sponsorship (account manager, coordinator)

- Ticketing and fan services (vice president, assistant director of sales, ticketing

Ticketing and fan services are just two of dozens of job areas for those seeking work in sports finance and administration. Here, ticket-takers deal directly with fans for a University of Tennessee football game.

manager, box office manager, new sales manager, season plan sales, group sales)

Several other departments more closely relate to administration, including communications and marketing, public relations, and community relations and promotions. Dozens of other jobs in the executive offices fall under the sports finance category as well.

MAJOR JOBS IN THE MINOR LEAGUES

Despite the keen interest in finance and administration careers at the highest levels of professional sports, the relatively small number of open positions and the resulting intense competition make it difficult for recent college graduates to land them. The Cleveland Indians human resources specialist who reported that he had received 1,500 applicants for six available internships added that even one part-time opening for a community outreach assistant—not one of the most sought-after jobs in major league sports—attracted 412 online applicants.

One should not be discouraged, however. Opportunities abound outside the NFL, NBA, NHL, and Major League Baseball. In fact, the minor league systems that support and feed these major leagues are significant enough to employ large numbers of sports finance and administration graduates. The NBA, NHL, and MLB all boast minor league systems that hone and promote talent not only on the court, field, and ice, but also in finance and administration.

A promotions and special events department's responsibility for entertaining fans goes far beyond the game itself these days. The Portland Sea Dogs stage mascot races between innings, allowing the fans to predict the winner and earn a prize.

The most extensive minor league system is in baseball. All thirty major league franchises operate between seven and nine minor league teams, from Rookie League to Triple-A. The highest-level minor league franchises, housed in comparatively large cities such as Columbus, Ohio; Memphis, Tennessee; Oklahoma City, Oklahoma; and Nashville, Tennessee, employ the greatest number of personnel in finance and administration. The Columbus Clippers, for instance, feature many of the same finance and administration departments as their major league affiliate, the Cleveland Indians, including ticket operations, ticket sales, marketing, finance, promotions, media relations, merchandising, group sales, and event planning.

The same holds true for the NHL, though its minor league system is not as extensive. Every NHL franchise operates an affiliate in the American Hockey League (AHL), and nearly all also have a lower-level team in the East Coast Hockey League (ECHL). Each of these minor league teams provide possible opportunities for younger job seekers in the field. One example is the AHL's Stockton Thunder, which employs a chief financial officer and director of corporate partnerships, as well as workers in outside sales, bookkeeping, group sales, marketing and business development, accounting, and ticket sales. All of these job areas fall under the umbrella of sports finance.

The NBA has developed two subsidiary league entities that offer hope for those looking to break into the industry. One is the Women's National Basketball Association (WNBA), which currently has franchises in twelve major cities, including New York, Chicago, and Los Angeles. The league offers realistic employment opportunities for young job seekers who prefer living in major metropolitan areas. In addition, the Developmental League, which is the only NBA minor league, boasts sixteen franchises, mostly in smaller cities throughout the country, with limited front office staff.

The large number of major league, minor league, and offshoot franchises in professional team sports offer consistent employment and internship opportunities for even the most inexperienced sports finance and administration prospects. The keys to securing one of these available spots are vigilance and an open mind. Those willing to scour franchise Web sites for openings, start a career in their professional specialty with a lower-level minor league team, relocate to a smaller city or regional center, or accept an entry-level, bottom-of-the-rung, "get your foot in the door" job with a major league team will find work more easily than those who set their sights too high. Those who are inflexible about the level of job, rank of team, or geographic location they will consider may find themselves out of work for an extended period of time.

OTHER OPPORTUNITIES IN PROFESSIONAL SPORTS

Baseball, football, basketball, and hockey are the four most popular sports in sports-crazed America, but they do not provide the only job possibilities at the professional level for those seeking a career in finance and administration. Far from it.

The most popular sport in the world is soccer—and it is finally picking up steam in the United States. The

Being willing to start at the bottom rung, develop a relationship with a mentor, build a network of professional contacts, and accept any and all responsibilities thrown your way will open up a clear path toward advancement in your field.

average attendance for a Major League Soccer (MLS) match in 2013 was more than eighteen thousand, with the Seattle Sounders easily leading the pack with more than forty-thousand fans in the stands per game. MLS teams attracted a higher average attendance than their counterparts in the NHL and NBA, though MLS teams generally play in venues with greater seating capacity.

Major League Soccer has sought for decades, with some success, to turn the huge popularity of American youth soccer into a larger fan base for the sport at the professional level. Marketing and pro-motions departments play a critical role in this cam-paign, which bodes well for future administrators special-izing in those fields. The Sounders, for instance, employ a

NASCAR has emerged as a hugely popular sport in the United States over the last few decades. It also enjoys some of the most lucrative corporate sponsorship deals. One of its biggest stars is Jimmie Johnson, seen here celebrating a victory.

director of youth development, director of camp programs, and a youth programs operations assistant, as well as many other jobs that fit the finance and administration mold.

Also battling for the sports entertainment dollar are leagues that promote less popular sports such as indoor football. The Arena Football League has attempted to take advantage of fans' thirst for the sport. Though professional football has blossomed into the most popular sport in America, the NFL season is the shortest of all major professional sports leagues, with the fewest games played. Arena Football plays its games in the late winter and spring months, capitalizing on a football fan base that goes into withdrawal during this period stretching from the conclusion of the Super Bowl to the college draft and the opening of NFL training camps. The indoor game is fast-paced and high-scoring, resulting in growing attendance figures. The average crowd for games in 2013 was nearly eight thousand.

Three of the most popular individual—as opposed to team—professional sports also provide career opportunities to sports finance and administration graduates. Organizations such as the Professional Golfers Association (PGA), Ladies Professional Golfers Association (LPGA), United States Golf Association (USGA), U.S. Association (USTA), Women's Tennis Association (WTA), and Professional Bowlers Association (PBA) all boast finance and administration specialists.

NEW KIDS ON THE BLOCK

The most popular sports in the United States in terms of television viewership and attendance have remained the same for decades. They are baseball, football, basketball, and hockey. This might never change. But one old sport and one new multisport activity have been rapidly gaining popularity since the turn of the twenty-first century. They are lacrosse and extreme sports.

Lacrosse is a fast-paced game in which players use sticks with webbed pockets at the head to pass and shoot a ball. They score by firing the ball past a goaltender into a net. In recent years, Major League Lacrosse has established itself as a viable entity, with franchises in several major metropolitan areas. Average attendance figures reach nearly ten thousand in such cities as Denver, Boston, and Baltimore. In 2013, the league office, which is based in Boston, listed jobs in accounting and finance, administration, communications/community relations, event management, and sales and marketing. Each of the eight franchises across the country feature finance and administration positions.

Extreme sports features various forms of high-risk skill sports that have been embraced by younger generations of athletes. These sports are featured in the Summer X Games and Winter X Games, annual events launched by the cable sports network ESPN to showcase sports such as bicycle motocross (BMX), skateboarding, snowboarding, and snowmobiling. The higher profile of extreme sports has turned skateboarders such as Tony Hawk and Shaun White (nicknamed "the Flying Tomato" for his flaming red hair) into stars of the American sports scene.

No sport enjoyed a more meteoric rise in interest in the 1990s and early 2000s than NASCAR (National Association of Stock Car Auto Racing). The average attendance of NASCAR events exploded to nearly 130,000 by 2005, before dropping to just less than 100,000 in 2012. The continued popularity has bolstered the number of front-office personnel at NASCAR. Many of its nineteen departments include employees who work in the realms of finance and administration, with an emphasis on marketing, promotions, and business development.

Different governing bodies represent the many styles of auto racing. Organizations such as the Indy Racing League and the U.S. Hot Rod Association (USHRA)all offer opportunities for recent college graduates to launch their careers in sports finance and administration. So do individual raceways around the country that seek to attract fans. The same holds true for horse racing, which also features several styles (including thoroughbred racing and harness racing) and governing bodies, as well as thousands of tracks across America.

All of the professional sports beyond baseball, football, basketball, and hockey give finance and administration career seekers a chance to make their mark in the sports for which they feel a passion. There is even a North American Tiddlywinks Association! Granted, employment opportunities in the smallest organizations might be limited, but those hiring will be impressed by an applicant's genuine interest and knowledge of their sport that few others might posses.

BIG MAN ON CAMPUS

While an extremely wide variety of professional sports leagues, associations, and teams employ finance and administration personnel, the same can be said about college sports. Those seeking work at the college level can search for jobs within the large governing bodies—the National Collegiate Athletic Association (NCAA) and the National Association of Intercollegiate Athletics (NAIA). They can also pursue careers within college conferences and athletic departments. The college sports landscape is peppered with more than one hundred conferences, including some that specialize in particular sports, and more than one thousand individual college athletic departments.

School membership in the NCAA, which is based in Indianapolis, Indiana, is divided into three divisions, based upon the college's size: Division I (the largest schools with the biggest athletic budgets), Division II, and Division III schools. The national office is structured into six departments, all of which employ personnel that fall into finance or administrative roles. Even the smaller NAIA, which is based in Kansas City,

Communications is a critical job at college athletic departments and leagues. Shown here is Bob Burda, who serves as associate commissioner/communications for the Big 12 Conference.

Missouri, boasts many directors and assistants who work in finance and administration. Some of their positions include:

- Vice president for administration and finance
- Vice president for marketing and communications
- Manager of legislative services
- Manager of development and corporate sponsorships
- Director of development and corporate sponsorships
- Manager of marketing and communications
- Director of eligibility services
- Manager of eligibility services
- Manager of communications and sports information
- Director of legislative services
- Controller (financial)
- Manager of marketing services
- Manager of development
- Director of communications and sports information

The vast amount of money at stake at the professional and college level of sports requires great care and attention to effectively manage and maximize. Just as with professional sports entities, the economic health of college conferences is dependent on the work of the chief financial officer (CFO). Big 12 Conference CFO Steve Pace explained his responsibilities in an interview with the author: "I make sure our financial reporting system functions to provide accurate, complete usable information for the users of the reports, like our administration, membership, and auditors," he says. "I train and supervise our accounting staff. I monitor the staff daily by reviewing their work and questioning their operations. I'm available to offer input to the [Big 12] Commissioner and Chief Operating Officer. I assist in developing research and drafting reports for a wide range of topics, such as employee benefits and TV revenue projections."

Many consider the chief financial officer the pinnacle of a career in sports finance, and, indeed, it takes years of training and perseverance to reach such a professional height. Pace honed his skills for thirteen years in a certified public accountant (CPA) firm in Dallas, Texas, before going on to serve as president of an accounting and management consulting firm in that same city.

The huge majority of employees in the sports finance and administration field will never become a chief financial officer. The goal for most is to reach a level of comfort and professional satisfaction in whatever job they find. And some of these jobs are in high school, middle school, or youth sports, where many in the world of finance and administration are making a difference for the youngest of athletes. Though this is the lowest level of sports in terms of athletic performance and professional compensation, it can offer the highest level of job satisfaction and impact.

Chapter 6

CAREERS AT THE HIGH SCHOOL, YOUTH, AND OLYMPIC LEVELS

The youth of America are the future of American athletics. While the driving force of many seeking a career in sports finance and administration is to be a part of the higher-profile professional and major college sports scenes, others are motivated by the opportunity to work at the grassroots level with the youngest athletes.

High school athletic directors and youth sports organizations help mold kids into better athletes and well-rounded individuals. In the professional and major college ranks, many in finance and administration toil behind the scenes and never come in contact with coaches and athletes. Such is not the case with high school athletic directors, who are the chief representatives of athletics at their institutions. They are not only responsible for the economic health of their departments, but also for interactions and relationship building among the athletes, coaches, teachers, parents, and student body at large. High school athletic directors are also the unofficial heads of public relations for their athletic departments.

A primary job for high school athletic directors is to ensure a wonderful experience for fans at sporting events, such as these students attending a high school homecoming football game in Montana.

DIVIDING YOUR ATTENTION
AND MULTITASKING

Jeff Cassella, who serves as athletic director at the sprawling Mentor High School in suburban Cleveland, understands these many duties as well as anyone. His high school is the most populous in Ohio. Mentor boasts twenty sports teams—at least six teams play in every season. He must not only schedule games in all of those sports, but he must also maintain strong relationships with the athletes, coaches, and parents involved in each of them. Cassella realizes that the most important sport to any given person is the one in which he or she—or his or her son or daughter—competes. So he must treat each sport with equal care, attention, and respect.

Though he knows that football brings in the most revenue, Cassella also understands that less popular sports still mean the world to the athletes and coaches who participate in them. So he gives them all his time, passion, and energy. "You must be flexible in this job," he says. "You must be willing to put the time in and be able to be in many places at once. You have to be a multitasker. Many different things are going on at the same time. Most importantly, you have to be a people person and a communicator. Ninety percent of this business is dealing with and working with people. You have to be good at that... The best part of the job is watching the athletes succeed.

High school athletic directors receive great satisfaction when a team wins a state championship. Mentor High School AD Jeff Cassella congratulates the members of Mentor's boys' basketball team, Ohio's Division I state champs.

Let's face it. Athletics is supposed to be an enjoyable experience. When they succeed, then I have done my job. When those lights come on Friday nights, there is no other feeling like it."

And when his Mentor boys basketball team captured the 2013 Ohio Division I state title, Cassella felt that all his hard work had paid off. He did not diagram one play or score one basket, but Cassella shared the joy of victory with the players and coaches. It is that jubilation and feeling of accomplishment that makes the job of athletic director so gratifying. "I felt great pride when we won the championship," he said. "You spend so much time doing this job that it is great to be rewarded. It was such an unbelievable experience. I will cherish every moment of it!"

Mentor High's basketball championship was sanctioned by the Ohio High School Athletic Association (OHSAA), which is the governing body of all high school sports in the state. Every state has its own athletic association, and they all employ personnel that fall under the finance and administration umbrella. The OHSAA is typical of high school sports governing organizations in that it employs a chief financial officer and several financial executives known as comptrollers. Among the administrators are commissioners and assistant commissioners responsible for everything from athlete eligibility requirements and corporate sponsorships to media and community relations.

SPORTS COAST-TO-COAST: CAREERS IN YOUTH AND OLYMPIC SPORTS

The popularity of youth sports in the United States extends far beyond high school football fields and basketball courts. Younger children throughout the country are involved in organized football, baseball, soccer, ice hockey, field hockey, lacrosse, softball, gymnastics, swimming, tennis, golf, ice skating, and other sports. Some are supported at the national level by such all-encompassing organizations as the National Alliance for Youth Sports. Other national groups such as Little League Baseball, Pop Warner football, and USA Gymnastics provide a more specific focus. And each sport is supported by many state and local organizations that provide funding, coaching, and venues for athletes of various ages and levels of talent.

One example is USA Swimming, based in Colorado Springs, Colorado. Its operations are detailed in *The Comprehensive Guide to Careers in Sports*, a book written by University of Massachusetts sports management professor Glenn M. Wong. He writes that the responsibilities of such organizations as USA Swimming extend far beyond the National Team. USA Swimming is also in charge of promoting the sport, aiding in the building of new aquatic centers, organizing swimming events, and managing its more than three hundred thousand members. Wong lists the departments involved in achieving the objectives of USA Swimming:

- **Business development:** acts as a promotions agency for the sport and organizes national events such as the U.S. Open and Olympic Trials

- **Business operations/member services:** manages the membership data for the organization's members; also manages the technology within the sport

OLYMPIC DOMINANCE

Those fortunate enough to land a job with the U.S. Olympic Committee, or any of its individual member organizations representing particular sports, are part of a glorious history. The American contingents have been the most successful in the world since the modern Summer Games were launched in 1896 and the Winter Olympics began in 1924.

The United States has participated in twenty-seven Summer Olympics. It has won a total of 2,400 medals, including 976 gold, more than double the totals earned by any other country. The Americans have also fared well in the Winter Olympics. Their total medal count of 253 in twenty-one Olympic Games ranks second to the 303 earned by Norway.

American achievement in the Olympic Games bodes well for the financial future of the American team. This, in turn, could mean more jobs in marketing, sales, and advertising with the USOC and its member organizations.

- **Club development:** assists with the planning and development of new aquatic centers

- **Financial affairs:** manages the organization's finances

- **National team:** prepares athletes and coaches for the highest level of international competition

- **Fund-raising and alumni:** acts as the fund-raising arm of USA Swimming

Those seeking work in sports finance and administration can focus on international amateur athletics and work for organizations like the USOC and its affiliates. Shown here is U.S. gymnast Kyla Ross performing in a World Championship event held in Belgium.

USA Swimming is typical of organizations that promote a particular sport and represent the amateur athletes who participate in it, from young children to— for those who prove dedicated and talented enough— American Olympians. These amateur athletic organizations offer employment possibilities at both the national and local levels for those seeking careers or who are already established in the industry.

These amateur athletic organizations are part of the overall structure that grooms, selects, and trains athletes for the Olympic Games. Those who yearn to be part of what many consider the greatest international sporting event in history should set their sights on working for the U.S. Olympic Committee or one of its dozens of affiliates, such as USA Swimming. The USOC, otherwise known as Team USA and based in Colorado Springs, Colorado, is not only dependent on the work of volunteers and interns. It also has a large full-time staff organized into several departments that employ finance and administration specialists. Some of the available job areas include accounts payable, communications, fund-raising, finance, fulfillment (donor thank-you gifts), marketing, and purchasing.

The USOC is the parent group to dozens of Winter and Summer Olympic sports organizations, the names of which all begin with "USA," such as USA Speedskating, USA Volleyball, and USA Archery. Each of these subsidiary organizations employs sports finance and administration professionals. Some of these employees once competed in the particular sport and continue to feel passion for it, a passion that now can be channeled into productive and lucrative work and a rewarding career.

FACILITY MANAGEMENT

Not all employers in sports finance and administration are organizations, schools, or events. Facilities that host athletic activities and events provide jobs for thousands of employees throughout the country. The busiest of these are stadiums and arenas in major cities that are not only home to professional franchises or major college teams, but also double as venues for concerts, circuses, ice shows, and other forms of entertainment for mass audiences.

These stadiums, arenas, and athletic facilities employ varying numbers of sports finance and administration specialists. A glance at the seventy-one employees listed in the online staff directory at TD Banknorth Garden in Boston (formerly known as the Boston Garden, home to the NHL's Boston Bruins and the NBA's Boston Celtics) reflects the extent and variety of positions available at such a venue. Twenty-five of the listed employees—more than one-third of the total—work in finance and administration. Twenty others are categorized as either marketing or sales specialists.

It is no surprise that facilities such as TD Banknorth Garden hire so many employees in finance and administration. Some arenas host 250 events or more every year, including forty-one regular-season games each for their

Sports facilities employ many in the realm of finance and administration. One of the newest facilities is the Barclays Center in New York, home of the NBA Brooklyn Nets and the host of many concerts, performances, and other special events.

NBA and NHL franchises. The most successful teams also play ten or more playoff games in winning seasons. The need for employees who can keep a facility's finances running smoothly is great: if the finances don't run smoothly, the facility's physical operations will soon stop running smoothly, as well.

SHOW ME THE MONEY

College graduates with a master's degree in business have a decision to make. Their love of sports might have motivated them to gear their education toward a career in sports finance and administration. But they also understand that it could take them longer to gain employment and earn competitive salaries in sports than in other areas of the business world. The competition for such jobs is fierce—there are

The money in professional sports trickles down from owners of sports teams such as Bob Kraft (*bottom, right*) of the New England Patriots, seen here sitting next to rock star Steven Tyler in the owner's box during a football game.

not many job openings, the number of college graduates seeking work in sports is high, and the salaries for starting positions, particularly with pro franchises, are comparatively low.

That is the bad news. The good news is that salaries in sports finance and administration rise substantially for those patient enough to remain in their jobs. Those who reach management levels can earn an income far above the norm for the average American worker. The following passage from a recent article in *Street & Smith's SportsBusiness Journal* listed the negatives for those seeking a job with a professional sports franchise: "Relatively low pay, particularly when compared with the starting salaries of most MBAs. Long hours. Lots of nights and weekends. Heavy on sales, especially at the start. Welcome to the lower rungs of a career ladder at a pro team."

The article goes on to offer a more rosy view, however, for those who stick it out and build a long-lasting career in sports finance and administration. Citing employment statistics gathered from 126 MLB, NFL, NBA, NHL, and MLS franchises, the article reveals that, though starting annual salaries range from $20,000 to $35,000, managers earn about $65,000 and directors boast average incomes of $105,000. The salaries rise to $165,000 for vice presidents and soar to $340,000 for senior and executive vice presidents. Salaries of up to $400,000 annually were reported for top executives.

There is nothing wrong with desiring and seeking great financial reward in sports finance and administration. But salary alone should never be the driving force behind career-related decisions. The prospect of working forty or more hours a week at a particular job precludes the notion that income alone is the most important factor. Those who do not enjoy their jobs are doomed to misery and quite possibly failure, even if they are highly paid. Only a combination of passion and aptitude for a vocation can ensure fulfillment and success. Indeed, the expression "money can't buy happiness" is as appropriate in sports finance and administration as it is in any career. Do it because you love it, and all other good things will follow.

COLLEGE AND UNIVERSITY PROGRAMS IN SPORTS ADMINISTRATION AND MANAGEMENT

The following is a list of colleges and universities that offer programs in sports administration and management (such programs are all-encompassing and include sports finance):

Arkansas State University
Jonesboro, Arkansas
Bachelor's degree in sports
    management

Ball State University
Muncie, Indiana
Bachelor's degree in sports
    administration

Baylor University
Waco, Texas
Master's degree in sports
    management

Bowling Green State
    University
Bowling Green, Ohio
Bachelor's and master's
    degrees in sports
    management

Columbia University
New York, New York
Master's degree in sports
    management

DePaul University
Chicago, Illinois
Master's degree in sports
    management

Drexel University
Philadelphia, Pennsylvania
Master's degree in sports
    management

Eastern Michigan
    University
Ypsilanti, Michigan
Master's degree in sports
    administration and
    sports science

Florida Atlantic University
Boca Raton, Florida
Master's degree in sports
management

Florida State University
Tallahassee, Florida
Bachelor's degree, master's
degree, and Ph.D. in
sports management

Georgetown University
Washington, D.C.
Master's degree in sports
management

Howard University
Washington, D.C.
Bachelor's degree in sports
management

Indiana State University
Terre Haute, Indiana
Bachelor's degree and master's degree in sports
management, recreation,
and youth leadership

Indiana University
Bloomington, Indiana
Bachelor's degree, master's
degree, and Ph.D. degree
in athletic administration and sports
management

Kent State University
Kent, Ohio
Bachelor's degree and master's degree in sports
administration and
sports and recreation
management

Kentucky Wesleyan University
Owensboro, KY
Bachelor's degree and master's degree in fitness and
sports management

Liberty University
Lynchburg, Virginia
Bachelor's degree and master's degree in sports
management

Louisiana State University
Baton Rouge, Louisiana
Bachelor's degree and master's degree in sports
management

Loyola University
Chicago, Illinois
Master's degree in sports
management

Michigan State University
East Lansing, Michigan
Master's degree in sports
administration

Minnesota State University
Mankato, Minnesota
Master's degree in sports
    management

Mississippi State University
Mississippi State, Mississippi
Master's degree in sports
    management

Missouri State University
Springfield, Missouri
Master's degree in sports
    management

New York University
New York, New York
Bachelor's degree in sports
    management

North Carolina State
    University
Raleigh, North Carolina
Bachelor's degree in sports
    management

Northwestern University
Chicago, Illinois
Master's degree in sports
    administration

Ohio State University
Columbus, Ohio
Masters's degree and Ph.D.
    in sports management

Ohio University
Athens, Ohio
Master's degree in athletic
    administration

Oklahoma State University
Stillwater, Oklahoma
Bachelor's degree in sports
    management and sports
    administration

Old Dominion University
Norfolk, Virginia
Bachelor's degree and mas-
    ter's degree in sports
    management

Purdue University
West Lafayette, Illinois
Master's degree in rec-
    reation and sports
    management

Rice University
Houston, Texas
Bachelor's degree in sports
    management

Rutgers University
New Brunswick, New Jersey
Bachelor's degree in sports
    management

San Diego State University
San Diego, California

Master's degree in sports
   business management

Seton Hall University
South Orange, New Jersey
Bachelor's degree and master's degree in sports
   management

Southern Methodist
   University
Dallas, Texas
Bachelor's degree and mas-
   ter's degree in sports
   management

St. Bonaventure University
St. Bonaventure, New York
Bachelor's degree in
   sports studies/sports
   management

St. Cloud State University
St. Cloud, Minnesota
Bachelor's degree in
   recreation/sports
   management

St. John's University
Queens, New York
Bachelor's degree and master's degree in sports
   management

Temple University
Philadelphia, Pennsylvania

Master's degree in sports
   and recreation
   management

Texas A&M University
College Station, Texas
Bachelor's degree, master's
   degree, and Ph.D. in
   sports management

University of Arkansas
Fayetteville, Arkansas
Bachelor's degree and master's degree in recreation
   and sports management

University of Connecticut
Storrs, Connecticut
Bachelor's degree, master's
   degree, and Ph.D. in
   sports management

University of Florida
Gainesville, Florida
Bachelor's degree, master's
   degree, and Ph.D. in
   sports management

University of Massachusetts
Amherst, Massachusetts
Bachelor's degree, master's
   degree, and Ph.D. in
   sports management

University of Michigan
Ann Arbor, Michigan

Bachelor's degree in sports management

University of North Carolina
Chapel Hill, North Carolina
Bachelor's degree in exercise and sports science/ sports administration

University of Ottawa
Ottawa, Ontario, Canada
Bachelor's degree, master's degree, and Ph.D. in sports management

University of San Francisco
San Francisco, California
Master's degree in sports management

University of Texas
Austin, Texas
Bachelor's degree, master's degree, and Ph.D. in sports management

University of Utah
Salt Lake City, Utah
Washington State University
Pullman, Washington
Master's degree in sports management

The following colleges offer online programs:

American Military University
Charles Town, West Virginia
Master's degree in sports management

American Public University
Charles Town, West Virginia
Master's degree in sports management, graduate certificate in sports management, and graduate certificate in athletic administration

Ashford University
Clinton, Iowa
Bachelor's degree in sports and recreation management

California University at Pennsylvania Online
California, Pennsylvania
Bachelor's degree in sports management; master's degree in sports management studies

Drexel University
Philadelphia, Pennsylvania
Master's degree in sports management

Full Sail University
Winter Park, Florida
Master's degree in sports
management

Grand Canyon University
Phoenix, Arizona
Bachelor's degree in business
administration-sports
management

Lasell College
Newtonville, Massachusetts
Master's degree in sports
management

Liberty University
Lynchburg, Virginia
Master's degree in sports
management

Northeastern University
Boston, Massachusetts
Master's degree in sports
leadership

Post University
Waterbury, Connecticut
Bachelor's degree in sports
management

Southern New Hampshire
University
Manchester, New
Hampshire

Bachelor's degree in sports
management

Southern New Hampshire
University Online
Manchester, New
Hampshire
Master's degree in sports
management

St. Leo University
St. Leo, Florida
Master's degree in sports
management

Tiffin University
Tiffin, Ohio
Bachelor's degree in business administration in
sports and recreation
management

A CAREER IN SPORTS FINANCE AND ADMINISTRATION AT A GLANCE

SIGNIFICANT POINTS

- Sports finance and administration involves the preparation and performing of economic and administrative tasks in helping to run an athletic franchise, department, facility, or event.

- Sports finance and administration exists at the high school, college, and professional levels, as well as in amateur levels from youth to Olympic.

- The owner is atop the hierarchy of any professional sports franchise. All major financial dealings made by the general manager and others must be approved by the owner.

- The athletic director (AD) runs both college and high school athletic departments. The AD is most often the only employee in a high school athletic department, but a major college AD is assisted by a wide array of economic-related departments, including ticket sales, compliance, finance, and accounting.

- Event and facility management are two sports-related jobs that finance and administration employment seekers can consider. The event manager and facility manager are the two chief executives in those positions, respectively.

EDUCATIONAL REQUIREMENTS

- A bachelor's degree in business, sports administration, or sports management is generally required to gain employment in most areas of sports finance and administration.

- Upper administrative positions with professional sports organizations, major college athletic departments, and prominent sports facilities most often require a master's degree in sports administration or sports management.

PREPARING FOR A CAREER

- Internships, summer jobs, and volunteer work in the field can prove critical to landing a job in sports finance and administration after graduation.

- College students should prepare a strong résumé, embark on a networking campaign, follow up with employers, be willing to relocate, and accept work at the bottom rung of an organization in order to launch a career and maximize employment potential.

- High school and college students should shadow their school's athletic director to learn the business from the inside.

STRUCTURE OF THE BUSINESS

- Among the many departments in a major college athletic office are administrators who work in marketing, promotions, advertising, media relations, and corporate sponsorships.

- Professional sports franchises boast dozens of finance-related jobs, starting at the top with the chief financial officer and controller, but also including specialists in business, merchandise sales, ticket sales, accounting, and many other jobs.

THINGS YOU SHOULD KNOW

- A salary cap restricts the amount of money that franchises in the National Basketball Association (NBA), National Football League (NFL), and National Hockey League (NHL) are allowed to spend on player salaries. Major League Baseball teams can spend as much as they wish but are taxed if they exceed a certain amount.

- Free agency allows professional athletes to market their services to any team, but it takes several years for players still desired by their original teams to reach that status.

FINDING A JOB

- Many organizations devoted to individual amateur sports also serve as the governing bodies of those sports, from the lowest youth levels to the Olympic levels. Jobs are often available at the national, state, and local levels within each of those organizations.

- Online sites have substantially raised the number of opportunities for job seekers to find openings in any sports franchise, organization, athletic department, facility, or event. All of these Web sites list job and even internship possibilities on their sites.

- Job sites such as Jobs in Sports and Teamworkonline.com, among others, can be subscribed to and utilized by those seeking work in the industry.

ACCOUNTANT

What Accountants Do: Accountants examine financial statements for accuracy and conformance with laws. They prepare and examine financial records. They ensure that financial records are accurate and that taxes are paid properly and on time. Accountants assess financial operations and work to help ensure that organizations run efficiently.

Duties: Accountants typically do the following:

- Examine financial statements to be sure that they are accurate and comply with laws and regulations

- Compute taxes owed, prepare tax returns, and ensure that taxes are paid properly and on time

- Inspect account books and accounting systems for efficiency and use of accepted accounting procedures

- Organize and maintain financial records

- Assess financial operations and make best practices recommendations to management

- Suggest ways to reduce costs, enhance revenues, and improve profits

In addition to examining and preparing financial documentation, accountants must explain their findings. This includes face-to-face meetings with organization managers and individual clients and preparing written reports.

Work Environment: Most accountants work full time. One in five work more than forty hours per week. Longer hours are typical at certain times of the year, such as at the end of the budget year or during tax season. Most accountants and auditors work in offices, although some work from home.

How to Become an Accountant: Most accountant positions require at least a bachelor's degree in accounting or a related field. Some employers prefer to hire applicants who have a master's degree, either in accounting or in business administration with a concentration in accounting.

A few universities and colleges offer specialized programs, such as a bachelor's degree in internal auditing. In some cases, graduates of community colleges, as well as bookkeepers and accounting clerks who meet the education and experience requirements set by their employers, get junior accounting positions and advance to accountant positions by showing their accounting skills on the job.

Work experience is important for getting a job, and most states require experience before an accountant can apply for a CPA license. Many colleges help students gain practical experience through summer or part-time internships with public accounting or business firms.

Every accountant filing a report with the Securities and Exchange Commission (SEC) is required by law to be a certified public accountant (CPA). Many other accountants choose to become a CPA to enhance their job prospects or to gain clients. CPAs are licensed by their state's board of accountancy. Becoming a CPA requires passing a national exam and meeting other state requirements.

Important Qualities:

- **Analytical skills:** Accountants and auditors must be able to identify issues in documentation and suggest solutions. For example, public accountants use analytical skills in their work to minimize tax liability, and internal auditors do so when identifying fraudulent use of funds.

- **Communication skills:** Accountants and auditors must be able to listen carefully to facts and concerns from clients, managers, and others. They must also be able to discuss the results of their work in both meetings and written reports.

- **Detail oriented:** Accountants and auditors must pay attention to detail when compiling and examining documentation.

- **Math skills:** Accountants must be able to analyze, compare, and interpret facts and figures, although complex math skills are not necessary.

- **Organizational skills:** Strong organizational skills are important for accountants and auditors who often work with a range of financial documents for a variety of clients.

Job Outlook: Employment of accountants and auditors is expected to grow 16 percent from 2010 to 2020, about as fast as the average for all occupations. There has been an increased focus on accounting in response to corporate scandals and recent financial crises. Stricter laws and regulations, particularly in the financial sector, will likely increase the demand for accounting services as organizations seek to comply with new standards. Additionally, tighter lending standards are expected to increase the importance of audits, as this is a key way for organizations to demonstrate their creditworthiness. The continued globalization of business should lead to more demand for accounting expertise and services related to international trade and international mergers and acquisitions.

Accountants and auditors who have earned professional recognition, especially as certified public accountants (CPA), should have the best prospects. Job applicants who have a master's degree in accounting or a master's degree in business with a concentration in accounting also may have an advantage. However, competition should be strong for jobs with the most prestigious accounting and business firms.

FINANCIAL MANAGERS

What Financial Managers Do: Financial managers perform data analysis and advise senior managers on profit-maximizing ideas. Financial managers are responsible for the financial health of an organization. They produce financial reports, direct investment activities, and develop strategies and plans for the long-term financial goals of their organization.

Duties: Financial managers typically do the following:

- Prepare financial statements, business activity reports, and forecasts

- Monitor financial details to ensure that legal requirements are met

- Supervise employees who do financial reporting and budgeting

- Review company financial reports and seek ways to reduce costs

- Analyze market trends to find opportunities for expansion or for acquiring other companies

- Help management make financial decisions

The following are examples of types of financial managers:

- **Controllers** direct the preparation of financial reports that summarize and forecast the organization's financial position, such as income statements, balance sheets, and analyses of future earnings or expenses. Controllers also are in charge of preparing special reports required by governmental agencies that regulate businesses. Often controllers oversee the accounting, audit, and budget departments.

- **Treasurers** and **finance officers** direct their organization's budgets to meet its financial goals. They oversee the investment of funds. They carry out strategies to raise capital (such as issuing stocks or bonds) to support the firm's expansion. They also develop financial plans for mergers (two companies joining together) and acquisitions (one company buying another).

- **Credit managers** oversee the firm's credit business. They set credit-rating criteria, determine credit ceilings, and monitor the collections of past-due accounts.

- **Cash managers** monitor and control the flow of cash that comes in and goes out of the company to meet the company's business and investment needs. For example, they must project cash flow (amounts coming in and going out) to determine whether the company will not have enough cash and will need a loan or will have more cash than needed and so can invest some of its money.

- **Risk managers** control financial risk by using hedging and other strategies to limit or offset the probability of a financial loss or a company's exposure to financial uncertainty. Among the risks they try to limit are those caused by currency or commodity price changes.

- **Insurance managers** decide how best to limit a company's losses by obtaining insurance against risks such as the need to make disability payments for an employee who gets hurt on the job and costs imposed by a lawsuit against the company.

Work Environment: Financial managers work closely with top managers and with departments that develop the data that financial managers need.

How to Become a Financial Manager: Financial managers must usually have a bachelor's degree and more than five years of experience in another business or financial occupation, such as loan officer, accountant, auditor, securities sales agent, or financial analyst. Many employers now seek candidates with a master's degree, preferably in business administration, finance, or economics. These academic programs help students develop analytical skills and learn financial analysis methods and software.

Important Qualities:

- **Analytical skills:** Financial managers increasingly assist executives in making decisions that affect the organization, a task for which they need analytical ability.

- **Communication skills:** Excellent communication skills are essential because financial managers must explain and justify complex financial transactions.

- **Detail oriented:** When preparing and analyzing reports such as balance sheets and income statements, financial managers must pay attention to detail.

- **Math skills:** Financial managers must be skilled in math, including algebra. An understanding of international finance and complex financial documents also is important.

- **Organizational skills:** Financial managers deal with a range of information and documents. They must stay organized to do their jobs effectively.

Job Outlook: Employment of financial managers in management of companies and enterprises is expected to grow by 3 percent from 2010 to 2020, slower than the average for all occupations. However, employment of self-employed financial managers is expected to grow at 20 percent from 2010 to 2020, faster than the average for all occupations.

As with other managerial occupations, job seekers are likely to face competition because the number of job openings is expected to be fewer than the number of applicants. Candidates with expertise in accounting and finance—particularly those with a master's degree or certification—should enjoy the best job prospects. An understanding of international finance and complex financial documents is important.

PUBLIC RELATIONS MANAGER AND SPECIALIST

What Public Relations Managers and Specialists Do: Public relations managers and specialists create and maintain a favorable public image for their employer or client. They write material for media releases, plan and direct public relations programs, and raise funds for their organizations.

Duties: Public relations managers and specialists typically do the following:

- Write press releases and prepare information for the media

- Identify main client groups and audiences and determine the best way to reach them

- Respond to requests for information from the media or designate an appropriate spokesperson or information source

- Help clients communicate effectively with the public

- Develop and maintain their organization's corporate image and identity, using logos and signs

- Draft speeches and arrange interviews for an organization's top executives

- Evaluate advertising and promotion programs to determine whether they are compatible with their organization's public relations efforts

- Develop and carry out fund-raising strategies for an organization by identifying and contacting potential donors and applying for grants

Work Environment: Public relations managers and specialists usually work in offices, but they also deliver speeches, attend meetings and community activities, and travel. They work in fairly high-stress environments, often managing and organizing several events at the same time. Most public relations managers and specialists work full time, which often includes long hours.

How to Become a Public Relations Manager or Specialist: For public relations management positions, a bachelor's degree in public relations, communications, or journalism is generally required. Courses in advertising, business administration, public affairs, public speaking, political science, and creative and technical writing are helpful. In addition, some employers prefer a master's degree in public relations or journalism. Currently, one-fourth of public relations managers hold a master's degree.

Public relations specialists typically are trained on the job, either in a formal program or by working closely under more experienced staff members. Entry-level workers often maintain files of material about an organization's activities, skim newspapers and magazines for appropriate articles to clip, and assemble information for speeches and pamphlets. Training typically lasts between one month and one year. After gaining experience, public relations specialists write news releases, speeches, and articles for publication. They also plan and carry out public relations programs.

Important Qualities:

- **Interpersonal skills:** Public relations managers and specialists deal with the public regularly, therefore they must be open and friendly in order to build rapport and get good cooperation from their media contacts.

- **Organizational skills:** Public relations managers and specialists are often in charge of managing several events at the same time, requiring superior organizational skills.

- **Good Judgment:** Public relations managers and specialists sometimes must explain how the company or client is handling sensitive issues. They must use good judgment in what they report and how they report it.

- **Research skills:** Public relations managers and specialists must often do research, including interviewing executives or other experts, to get the information they need.

- **Speaking skills:** Public relations managers and specialists regularly speak on behalf of their organization. When doing so, they must be able to explain the organization's position clearly.

- **Writing skills:** Public relations managers and specialists must be able to write well-organized and clear press releases and speeches. They must be able to grasp the key messages they want to get across and write them in a short, succinct way to get the attention of busy readers or listeners.

Job Outlook: Employment of public relations managers is expected to grow 21 percent from 2010 to 2020, faster than the average for all occupations. Employment of public relations specialists is expected to grow 23 percent during the same period, faster than the average for all occupations. Employment of public relations managers is expected to grow 16 percent from 2010 to 2020, about as fast as the average for all occupations. The trends affecting public relations specialists will also affect managers, as the increasing importance of public relations will require more managers to plan and direct public relations departments.

Organizations are increasingly emphasizing community outreach and customer relations as a way to enhance their reputation and visibility. Public opinion can change quickly, particularly because both good and bad news spreads rapidly through the Internet. Consequently, public relations specialists are expected to be needed to respond to news developments and maintain their organization's reputation.

Increased use of social media also is expected to increase employment growth for public relations specialists. These new media outlets will create more work for public relations workers, increasing the number and kinds of avenues of communication between organizations and the public. Public relations specialists will be needed to help their clients use these new types of media effectively.

Employment is likely to grow in public relations firms as organizations contract out public relations services rather than support more full-time staff when additional work is needed.

GLOSSARY

accounting The job of setting up, maintaining, and analyzing the financial records of a business.

alumni The graduates of a particular high school or college.

amateur An individual who is not paid for his or her work in an activity or sport.

athletic director The head of a high school or college athletic department.

booster A person who contributes money to an athletic program.

budget An estimate of income and expense for a future period of time.

chief financial officer (CFO) The person most responsible for the financial dealings of a business entity.

community relations A department that works toward establishing and maintaining a strong working relationship with the community in which a team is based and plays its home games.

controller An employee who keeps tabs on finances; a controller often works under the CFO.

corporate partnership A working relationship between a sports entity and a local business that features mutually beneficial advertising, marketing, promotions, and special events.

free agent An athlete who is free to market his or her services to any team.

fund-raiser Any number of events, generally at the high school or youth sports level, designed to raise money for the operations of an athletic program, including uniforms, equipment, facility and field maintenance, salaries, and travel expenses.

hierarchy A system or organization in which people or groups are ranked one above the other according to status or authority.

internship Generally unpaid or low-paid work that allows the participant to gain professional experience in a particular field.

interview A conversation between an employer and prospective employee in which the former asks questions of the latter to determine if the latter should be hired.

lucrative Profitable; moneymaking.

marketing Activities performed in an attempt to convince others to purchase a product.

merchandising The selling of goods related to a sports franchise or athletic department.

National Collegiate Athletic Association (NCAA) The primary governing body of college sports.

negotiation Discussion aimed at reaching an agreement, such as on a player's contract.

networking Using the help of associates to reach a goal, such as landing a job.

payroll The total amount of employees' salary within a company or organization.

professional An individual who is paid to work and perform a certain job.

reference A person whose name and contact information is provided by a job seeker; if contacted by a potential employer, the reference would be expected to provide information about the job applicant's work habits, abilities, skills, potential, personality, and experience.

relocation Leaving home to take a job elsewhere.

résumé A brief written account of past academic and work experience and achievements used to convince employers to hire a prospective employee.

revenue The amount of money coming in to a business.

salary cap The total amount of money a sports league allows teams to pay its players during the course of a season.

scholarship Tuition offered by athletic departments to talented athletes in an attempt to lure them to their school.

shadowing Following an employee to learn about what he or she does in his or her job.

undergraduate Any college student who has not yet graduated and received a bachelor's degree.

venue A place where a sporting event is played, such as an arena or stadium.

FOR MORE INFORMATION

Amateur Athletic Union
1910 Hotel Plaza Boulevard
Lake Buena Vista, FL 32830
(407) 934-7200
Web site: http://www.aausports.org
This organization serves to further the cause of amateur
sports. It publicizes events and supports amateur
athletics through local clubs.

AthletesCan: The Association of Canada's National Team
Athletes
1376 Bank Street, Suite 301
Ottawa, ON K1H 7Y3
Canada
(613) 526-4025
Web site: http://athletescan.com
This group supports and provides information about
Canadian athletes.

International Ticketing Association
Two Meridian Plaza
10401 North Meridian Street, Suite 300
Indianapolis, IN 46290
(212) 629-4036
This nonprofit organization serves as a forum to aid ticketing professionals in the sports and entertainment
businesses.

Little League Baseball and Softball
595 U.S. 15
Williamsport, PA 17702
(570) 326-1921
Web site: http://www.littleleague.org/Little_League_
    Online.htm
This organization supports the players, parents, coaches,
    and umpires involved in Little League baseball and
    softball throughout the United States.

National Alliance for Youth Sports
National Headquarters
2050 Vista Parkway
West Palm Beach, FL 33411
(561) 684-1141
Web site: http://www.nays.org
This organization trains and aids volunteer youth sports
    administrators and coaches.

National Association for Collegiate Directors of America
    (NACDA)
24651 Detroit Road
Westlake, OH 44145
(440) 892-4000
Web site: http://www.nacda.com
This group provides support for and information about
    college athletic directors.

National Association of Collegiate Women Athletics
    Administrators (NACWAA)
2000 Baltimore Avenue
Kansas City, MO 64108
(816) 389-8200

Web site: http://nacwaa.org
This organization provides support and an online career center for administrators and job seekers in women's college sports.

National Association of Girls and Women in Sport (NAGWS)
1900 Association Drive
Reston, VA 20191
(703) 476-3453
Web site: http://www/aahperd.org
This group supports women's athletics through its publications, internships, and career information.

National Collegiate Athletic Association (NCAA)
700 West Washington Street
P.O. Box 6222
Indianapolis, IN 462060-6222
(317) 917-6222
Web site: http://www.ncaa.org
This governing body provides resources, news, and information about college sports.

National Interscholastic Athletic Administrators Association (NIAAA)
9100 Keystone Crossing, Suite 650
Indianapolis, IN 46240
(317) 587-1450
Web site: http://www.niaaa.org
This organization promotes the ideals of American high school sports.

North American Society for Sport Management
135 Winterwood Drive

Butler, PA 16001
(724) 482-6277
Web site: http://www.nassm.com
This organization supports sports management professionals through the promotion of research, writing, and
development.

Sport Canada
15 Eddy Street, 16th Floor
Gatineau, QC K1A 0M5
Canada
(819) 997-0155
Web site: http://pch.gc.ca/eng/1268160670172
/1268160761399
This group is the single largest investor in the Canadian
sports system and seeks to aid amateur athletes in that
country.

Sports Financial Advisors Association
10645 North Tatum Boulevard, Suite 200–608
Phoenix, AZ 85028
(602) 820-2220
Web site: http://www.sportsfinancial.org
This organization is dedicated to providing financial advice
and aid to a wide array of professionals in the sports
industry.

Sports Management Worldwide
1100 NW Glisan Street, Suite 2B
Portland, OR 97209
(877) 769-9669
Web site: http://www.smwwagency.com
This company connects athletes, agents, teams, and sponsorships throughout the world.

U.S. Olympic Committee (USOC)
27 South Tejon
Colorado Springs, CO 80903
(888) 222-2313
Web site: http://www.teamusa.org
This group supports United States Olympic and Paralympic
    athletes in their quest for sustained excellence.

WEB SITES

Due to the changing nature of Internet links, Rosen Publishing has developed an online list of Web sites related to the subject of this book. This site is updated regularly. Please use this link to access the list:

http://www.rosenlinks.com/GCSI/Fin

FOR FURTHER READING

Ammon, Robin, Richard M. Southall, and Mark S. Nagel. *Sport Facility Management: Organizing Events and Mitigating Risks*. Morgantown, WV: Fitness Information Technology, 2010.

Bill, Karen. *Sport Management*. Exeter, England: Learning Matters, 2009.

Brown, Matthew T., Daniel A. Rascher, Chad D. McEvoy, and Mark S. Nagel. *Financial Management in the Sports Industry*. Scottsdale, AZ: Holcomb Hathaway Publishers, 2010.

Coakley, Jay. *Sports in Society: Issues and Controversies*. New York, NY: McGraw-Hill, 2008.

DeSensi, Joy Theresa, and Danny Rosenberg. *Ethics and Morality in Sport Management*. Morgantown, WV: Fitness Information Technology, 2010.

Devantier, Alecia T., and Carol A. Turkington. *Extraordinary Jobs in Sports*. New York, NY: Facts On File, 2006.

Favorito, Joseph. *Sports Management in Practice—Sport Publicity: A Practical Approach*. Burlington, MA: Butterworth-Heinemann, 2007.

Ferguson Publishing. *Ferguson's Careers in Focus: Sports*. New York, NY: Facts On File, 2005.

Field, Shelly. *Managing Your Career in the Sports Industry*. New York, NY: Checkmark Books, 2008.

Finch, Jennie, and Ann Killion. *Throw Like a Girl: How to Dream Big and Believe in Yourself*. Chicago, IL: Triumph Books, 2011.

Fried, Gil. *Managing Sports Facilities*. Champaign, IL: Human Kinetics, 2009.

Fried, Gil, et al. *Sports Finance.* 3rd Ed. Champaign, IL: Human Kinetics, 2013.

Greenwald, John. *Field Guides to Finding a New Career: Sports Industry.* New York, NY: Ferguson Publishing, 2010.

Heitzmann, Ray. *Careers for Sports Nuts & Other Athletic Types.* New York, NY: McGraw-Hill, 2004.

Hopwood, Maria, James Skinner, and Paul Kitchin. *Sport Public Relations and Communication.* Burlington, MA: Elsevier, 2010.

Howell, Brian. *Sports* (Inside the Industry). San Francisco, CA: Essential Library, 2011.

Hunter, Nick. *Money in Sports* (Ethics of Sports). Chicago, IL: Heinemann Library, 2012.

Kelley, David J. *Sports Fundraising: Dynamic Methods for Schools, Universities, and Youth Sports Organizations.* New York, NY: Routledge, 2012.

McKinney, Ann. *Real Résumés for Sports Industry Jobs: Including Real Résumés Used to Change Careers and Gain Federal Employment.* Fayetteville, NC: Prep Publishing, 2004.

McLeish, Ewan. *Sports Industry* (A Closer Look: Global Industries). New York, NY: Rosen Publishing, 2011.

Mullin, Bernard, Stephen Hardy, and William Sutton. *Sports Marketing.* Champaign, IL: Human Kinetics, 2007.

National Interscholastic Athletic Administrators Association. *NAIII's Guide to Interscholastic Athletic Administration.* Champaign, IL: Human Kinetics, 2013.

Pratt, Ancel R. *Jewels of the Game—How to Get a Job Working in Sports.* Raleigh, NC: Lulu.com, 2011.

Reeves, Diana Lindsey. *Career Ideas for Kids Who Like Sports.* New York, NY: Checkmark Books, 2007.

Schaaf, Phil. *Sports, Inc.: 100 Years of Sports Business.* Amherst, NY: Prometheus Books, 2003.

Schultz, Christian Dahl. *Ferguson Career Launcher: Professional Sports Organizations.* New York, NY: Ferguson Publishing, 2011.

Trenberth, Linda, and David Hassan, eds. *Managing Sports Business: An Introduction*. London, England: Routledge, 2011.

Watt, David. *Sports Management and Administration*. London, England: Routledge, 2003.

Wells, Michelle, Andy Kreutzer, and Jim Kahler. *A Career in Sports: Advice from Sports Business Leaders*. Livonia, MI: M. Wells Enterprises, 2010.

Winfree, Jason A., and Mark S. Rosentraub. *Sports Finance and Management: Real Estate, Entertainment, and the Remaking of the Business*. Boca Raton, FL: CRC Press, 2011.

BIBLIOGRAPHY

Associated Press. "Average Salary Hits $3.2M." ESPN.com, December 7, 2012. Retrieved August 2013 (http://espn .go.com/mlb/story/_/id/8724285/mlb-average-salary- 38-percent-32-million).

Battle, Bill. Interview with the author. Conducted July 12, 2013.

Bureau of Labor Statistics. "Accountants and Auditors." *Occupational Outlook Handbook*, August 31, 2012. Retrieved December 2013 (http://www.bls.gov/ooh /Business-and-Financial/Accountants-and-auditors.htm).

Bureau of Labor Statistics. "Financial Managers." *Occupational Outlook Handbook*, March 29, 2012. Retrieved December 2013 (http://www.bls.gov/ooh /Management/Financial-managers.htm).

Bureau of Labor Statistics. "Public Relations Managers and Specialists." *Occupational Outlook Handbook*, March 29, 2012. Retrieved December 2013 (http://www.bls.gov /ooh/Management/Public-relations-managers-and- specialists.htm).

Casagrande, Michael. "Al Golden: Let's Put an NCAA Compliance Officer on Every Campus." *Sun-Sentinel*, July 30, 2013. Retrieved August 2013 (http://www .sun-sentinel.com/sports/um-hurricanes/miami- hurricanes-blog/sfl-al-golden-lets-put-an-ncaa- compliance-officer-on-every-campus-20130730, 0,1813470.post).

Cassella, Jeff. Interview with the author. Conducted July 9, 2013.

Culpepper, Pat. "Nothing Like Texas High School Football!" *Cleburne Eagle News*, June 10, 2010. Retrieved July 2013 (http://cleburneeaglenews.com/nothing-like-texas-high -school-football-p251.htm).

Dickestel.com. "National Hockey League Minor League Affiliations." September 2, 2012. Retrieved August 2013 (http://www.dickestel.com/hockeyaffil.htm).

Dietl, Helmut, Markus Lang, and Stephan Werner. "The Effect of Luxury Taxes on Competitive Balance, Club Profits, and Social Welfare in Sports Leagues." North American Association of Sports Economists, August 2008. Retrieved July 2013 (http://college.holycross.edu /RePEc/spe/DietlLangWerner_LuxuryTaxes.pdf).

Field, Shelly. *Career Opportunities in the Sports Industry*. New York, NY: Checkmark Books, 2010.

Fried, Gil, Steven Shapiro, and Timothy D. Deschriver. *Sports Finance*. Champaign, IL: Human Kinetics, 2007.

High School Baseball Web. "NCAA Scholarships by Sport." Retrieved July 2013 (http://www.hsbaseballweb.com /scholarships_by_sport.htm).

IBM. "Data Sets: Average NFL Salary ($10,000s) by Year." April 16, 2012. Retrieved August 2013 (http://www -958.ibm.com/software/analytics/manyeyes/datasets/ average-nfl-salary-10000s-by-year/versions/1).

Kellogg, Brady. Interview with the author. Conducted June 11, 2013.

King, Bill. "What's the Payoff in Sports?" *Street & Smith's SportsBusiness*, August 13, 2012. Retrieved August 2013 (http://www.sportsbusinessdaily.com/Journal/Issues /2012/08/13/In-Depth/Salary-survey.aspx).

Liebman, Glenn. "5 Quotes by Legendary Texas Coach Darrell Royal." ESPN. Retrieved August 42013 (http:// espn.go.com/espn/page2/index?id=5639164).

Lindstrom, Erick, and Erika K. Arroyo. *Sports* (Discovering Careers). New York, NY: Facts On File, 2010.

Major League Baseball Players Association. "Average Salaries in Major League Baseball: 1967-2009." Retrieved August 2013 (http://hosted.ap.org/specials/interactives /_sports/baseball08/documents/bbo_average_salary 2009.pdf).

Major League Lacrosse. "Careers." Retrieved August 2013 (http://majorleaguelacrosse.teamworkonline.com/ teamwork/jobs/default.cfmnaia.org).

Mataconis, Doug. "Texas High School Builds $60 Million Football Stadium." OutsidetheBeltway.com. Retrieved July 2013 (http://www.outsidethebeltway.com/texas-high-school-builds-60-million-football-stadium).

NBA.com. "NBA Career Opportunities." Retrieved August 2013 (http://careers.peopleclick.com/careerscp/client_ nba/external/search.do).

Northwestern University. "Career Options: Sports Administration." Retrieved July 2013 (http://www.scs .northwestern.edu/program-areas/graduate/sports-administration/career-options.php).

Ohio University College of Business. "Sports Management." Retrieved July 2013 (http://aspnet.cob.ohio.edu/isms/ cobContent.aspx?4805).

Pace, Steve. Interview with the author. Conducted August 1, 2013.

Rhoden, William C. "University Compliance Officers: Good Cop, Bad Cop." *New York Times*, April 10, 2009. Retrieved August 2013 (http://www.nytimes. com/2009/04/11/sports/ncaabasketball/11rhoden.html).

Shipley, Amy. "United States Wins the Medal Count at Vancouver Olympics with a Record 37, and the Impact Will Last into the Future." *Washington Post*, March 1, 2010. Retrieved August 2013 (http://www.washington post.com/wp-dyn/content/article/2010/02/28/AR201 0022803290.html).

Stockton Thunder. "Staff Directory." Retrieved August 2013 (http://www.stocktonthunder.com/team/front-office).

Summer at Georgetown: Summer Programs for High School Students. "Sports Industry Management." Retrieved July 2013 (http://scs.georgetown.edu/programs/112/summer-programs-for-high-school-students-sports-industry-management).

TD Banknorth Garden. "Company Directory of Business Contacts." Retrieved August 2013 (https://connect.data.com/directory/company/list/173100/td-banknorth-garden?guid=173100).

Wecker, Menachem. "M.B.A. Is MVP of Sports Management Industry, Some Say." *U.S. News & World Report*, December 22, 2011. Retrieved July 2013 (http://www.usnews.com/education/best-graduate-schools/top-business-schools/articles/2011/12/22/mba-is-mvp-of-sports-management-industry-some-say).

Wharton: University of Pennsylvania. "Wharton Sports Business Academy." Retrieved July 2013 (http://www.wharton.upenn.edu/academics/sports-business-academy.cfm).

Wong, Glenn M. *The Comprehensive Guide to Careers in Sports*. Sudbury, MA: Jones & Bartlett, 2008.

INDEX

ABOUT THE AUTHOR

Marty Gitlin is an educational book writer and sportswriter based in Cleveland, Ohio. He has had more than seventy-five books published, many in the sports realm. During his twenty-five years as a newspaper sportswriter, he won more than forty-five awards, including first place for general excellence from the Associated Press for his coverage of the 1995 World Series. That organization also selected him as one of the top four feature writers in Ohio in 2001. Gitlin covered the Cleveland Browns for CBSsports.com from 2009 to 2012 before becoming a fantasy football and baseball writer for that Web site in 2013.

PHOTO CREDITS

Cover, p. 1 (figure) © iStockphoto.com/Ljupco; cover, p. 1 (arena) © iStockphoto.com/ZargonDesign; pp. 4–5 RJ Sangosti/Denver Post/Getty Images; p. 10 Joe Robbins/Getty Images; pp. 12, 13, 17, 24, 43, 55, 86–87, 96–97, 98–99 © AP Images; p. 20 Kazuhiro Nogi/AFP/Getty Images; p. 29 Goodluz/Shutterstock.com; p. 30 © University of South Carolina Athletics; p. 32 Al Tielemans/Sports Illustrated/Getty Images; p. 36 Eric Francis/Getty Images; p. 39 (bottom) Ohio University Center for Sports Administration; p. 46 Spencer Platt/Getty Images; pp. 48, 70 © Wade Rackley/Tennessee Athletics; p. 50 © iStockphoto.com/vm; p. 57 © Syracuse Newspapers/J Berry/The Image Works; p. 59 Chris Condon/US PGA Tour/Getty Images; p. 63 Angels Baseball; p. 67 Image Source/Stockbyte/Getty Images; pp. 72–73 Portland Sea Dogs; p. 75 iStock/Thinkstock; pp. 76–77 Tom Pennington/NASCAR/Getty Images; p. 82 © Big 12 Conference; p. 89 © Mentor High School; p. 93 John Thys/AFP/Getty Images; interior design elements (graph) © iStockphoto.com/hudiemm, (stripes) Lost & Taken; pp. 9, 27, 39 (top), 54, 66, 86, 101, 107, 111, 125, 128, 133, 136, 140; © iStockphoto.com unless otherwise noted. From top left ultramarinfoto, Kayann, VIPDesignUSA, plherrera, cb34inc, yai112, Jimmy Anderson, dbrskinner, dswebb, Gannet77, Sergieiev/Shutterstock.com, gzaleckas, choja, cscredon, peepo.

Designer: Nicole Russo; Photo Researcher: Marty Levick